HOW TO RAISE CHRISTIAN KIDS
—IN A—
NON-CHRISTIAN WORLD

HOW TO RAISE CHRISTIAN KIDS
IN A
NON-CHRISTIAN WORLD

VICTOR BOOKS®

A DIVISION OF SCRIPTURE PRESS PUBLICATIONS INC.
USA CANADA ENGLAND

All material in this book is excerpted from *Parents & Teenagers,* © 1984 by Youth for Christ/USA and *Parents & Children,* © 1986 by Youth for Christ/USA.

Bible quotations in this book are from: the *King James Version* (KJV); the *New American Standard Bible* (NASB), © the Lockman Foundation 1960, 1962, 1963, 1968, 1971, 1972, 1973, 1975, 1977; and the *Holy Bible, New International Version* (NIV), © 1973, 1978, 1984, International Bible Society. Used by permission of Zondervan Bible Publishers.

Recommended Dewey Decimal Classification: 155.4-155.5
Suggested Subject Heading: CHILDREN—TRAINING

Library of Congress Catalog Card Number: 87-62481
ISBN: 0-89693-468-3

© 1988 by Youth for Christ/USA. All rights reserved
Printed in the United States of America

C O N T E N T S

With appreciation to the following men and women who contributed their parenting wisdom to this book:

Bruce & Mitzie Barton
V. Gilbert Beers
B. Clayton Bell
Bill Bright
Ross Campbell
Anthony Campolo
Evelyn Christenson
Donald & Naomi Cole
Jim & Sally Conway
Mark Cosgrove
James Dobson
Byron Emmert
Leighton Ford
James Galvin
Kenneth Gangel
Dick Hagstrom
Richard Halverson
Tim Hansel
Paul Heidebrecht
Howard Hendricks
Harvey Hook

Ronald Hutchcraft
Jay Kesler
Grace Ketterman
Paul Kienel
Larry Kreider
Marlene LeFever
David & Karen Mains
Josh McDowell
Gregory Monaco
Ronald Nikkel
Paul & Virginia Nurmi
Larry Richards
Adrian Rogers
Barry St. Clair
Cliff Schimmels
Timothy Skrivan
Charles Swindoll
David & Gail Veerman
John Whitehead
Warren Wiersbe
H. Norman Wright

INTRODUCTION

The modern world has become a complex place in which to live. It is no longer easy to make some of the moral decisions that were made routinely as recently as a generation ago.

Television is in almost every home. Movies of all kinds are available. Music floods the airways. Young people are constantly bombarded with things that would have made their grandparents blush.

As parents, we must face these problems head-on. We must teach our young people how to distinguish between right and wrong without raising them in an atmosphere of legalism.

Legalism—going to a rule book for answers to every situation—is attractive because of its certainty, but it is too simple. It does not take all the facts into consideration. And its interpretations of the world tend to let people down when they run into real problems.

Part of our Christian responsibility is helping our kids find the best. And the best must take into consideration not only the history of civilization and human learning, but also the revelation given to us by God in Scripture. Only God can give us the very best.

Jay Kesler

C H A P T E R
1

How Do
I Handle Society's Attack
on My Family?

Are You Equipped for the Attack?
JOHN WHITEHEAD

THE FAMILY, A ONCE REVERED INSTITUTION IN OUR COUNTRY, is under tremendous attack today. During the past forty years, we have seen a significant decline in what we call the traditional family, and I believe much of the problem is of a spiritual nature. Some Christian counselors tell me that 50 percent of the Christian marriages in their areas end in divorce. As a result, many children are now living in single-parent homes, foster homes, state centers, and orphanages.

However, I believe the trends of the past couple of years indicate a resurgence of the Christian family. People are having more children, and I think families are going to get stronger. But there are still a number of influences in our society that are having a negative effect on today's families.

The strong *feminist movement* is one negative influence on the family. In many ways, this movement tends to be anti-family, primarily due to its pro-abortion attitude.

Another influence with which the family has to contend is the *media.* Television presents a one-sided view of the family—mostly bad. Almost all of the programs are aimed at singles; there are very few family shows. Even a lot of the early TV shows were centered on one-parent families—"Andy Griffith" and "Lassie," for example. Other programs are excessively violent or just plain anti-Christian.

I'll probably get criticized for including this third negative family influence on my list, but I think that *excessive church activities* can often be so demanding that parents don't have time to spend with their children. Churches should encourage families to get together at nighttime and have devotionals or do something as a group. But I've seen many churches plan so many activities for parents and children that they are rarely together at home.

Parents who don't spend time with their children miss a very special relationship. Yet some people tend to think it's more spiritual to spend every spare minute plugged into a church activity than to lie around on the carpet at home and play with their children. Strong family relationships just can't be developed if part of the family is *always* at church for one reason or another.

If you want to develop better relationships with your children, it's always good to identify any negative influences of society you see in your family situation. But it isn't enough to identify them—you must do something about them.

For instance, if TV is a major problem, turn it off. We have very limited viewing in our family. We watch only what we feel to be wholesome shows, and we either watch them *with* our children or *before* we allow them to watch.

TV can be used in an educational way. What we do with our children is tell them what is happening in the world (such topics as abortion or evolution) and then watch shows and read books that deal with those issues. By the time my son was in third grade, I had taught him the basic catch words for evolutionary thinking, and he could watch a show and tell me if it was promoting evolution even if the word *evolution* was never used. He could tell that a discussion on "adaptation," for example, was actually on evolution and went against the creationist beliefs he had been taught. If you take the time to educate your children about other worldviews, they will filter out a lot of television programs through their "Christian screen" without any further instructions on your part.

It is good to help your teens practice using their Christian screen. After a TV show or movie, my teenager and I frequently sit down together and discuss what we have just seen from a Christian worldview. What was the message of the program? What moral problems were raised on the show? How would you resolve them? Was the main character's method of resolution a good one to imitate?

This type of education must be taught in the homes by the parents, not in the schools. As the parents work with their teens to develop a Christian worldview, many of society's negative influences can be overcome. You probably won't get rid of all of them, but you will start your children in the right direction.

Another example I can use from my own experience is rock music. I'm not saying all rock is bad, but few will argue that some rock music is a very bad influence. Our thirteen-year-old began to learn classical guitar about four or five years ago, and he became familiar with classical music. Sometimes we will put on a rock record, listen to it, and discuss it. Many times he will say, "I don't want to listen to that song because it isn't orderly. It doesn't fit in with the scheme of music." If you expose your children to the right influences, they will soon begin to filter out a lot of the wrong ones by themselves.

Our nation is facing a horrible moral crisis today. If we are to have revival, reformation, or whatever you want to call it, the reform must come through two channels. The main burden is on the church, though I think the church has failed in our country in recent years. The other avenue for reform is the family, the basic institution of society. When America had strong families, America was strong morally. Religion is a product of the family. If a child is not taught religion in his home, he probably will not be religious.

The church where we are members is a place we go to worship with other Christians. But we are taught there that the primary worship center is the home. Christians today have a false idea of what worship is all about. Worship involves more than attending church or handing out tracts. It means doing the best you can at whatever you are doing, and being the best person you can be. We are commanded to let our lights shine before men, and there are many ways we can do that.

Parents should make sure their lights shine at home. Family Bible reading is a good place to start. By the time my oldest son was eleven, he had already read the King James Bible from cover to cover with us. By the time a child is able to read, he should be encouraged to participate in family devotions.

Our family also uses devotional books. We particularly like one called *Timeless Insights*. But we emphasize Bible reading. I have found that most Christians haven't read the Bible cover to cover, and that's a problem that can be dealt with in the homes.

Of course, you're going to have some problems with your children. We don't live in a fairyland. Society's assault on the family is real. But as parents begin to recognize and attend to the problems their children are facing, they can successfully counteract the negative influences their teens encounter every day.

Should Parents Protect Their Children from Negative Influences?
DONALD COLE

SOME PEOPLE SAY THAT YOU CANNOT PROTECT YOUR teenagers from negative influences. To a certain extent that is true. You can't protect them from all negative influences, but you certainly can protect them from many, and you should, even when they are teenagers.

A typical teenager is not prepared to cope with many of the temptations that come his way. Temptations don't simply sneak up on you in this modern world. They come vacuum-packed, under great pressure. A teenager who is not given support may succumb when, under better circumstances, he might stand firm.

I'm not saying that you should keep your kids isolated from the realities of the world. They should be prepared for what they will face. But part of that preparation is protection from assault before they are equipped to meet it.

I try to keep my kids from seeing pornography because I do not believe that any person can be exposed to pornography without having his mind permanently affected.

The same holds true for dirty books. Anything that is degrading should be kept away from children. The lie of the devil is that experience will make you wiser. The fact is that experience may destroy you if you are not mature enough to handle it. The devil says that sexual experimentation is OK because once you've done it, somehow you've matured. But it doesn't work that way.

I also think that kids should not be allowed to watch X-rated movies. My responsibility as a parent is to protect them. The yardstick is: Would I expose my fourteen- 'or fifteen-year-old daughter to a thirty-year-old man whom I suspected of wanting to seduce her? No, I'd protect her from that. I'd also protect her from seeing that in a movie.

I would also do my best to keep comic books out of their hands. The reason is quite simple: I want them to learn to appreciate literature. Once they have developed a taste for literature, they are not going to read junk.

As for teen music, some of the words and music are plain rotten. You may not be able to prevent your kids from listening to it somewhere, but you can keep it out of your home. I do not think that a Christian has to be so tolerant and liberal that he has it in his home.

A record that has suggestive lyrics will not find a place in my home. You may cultivate in your children a certain amount of resentment, but that will resolve itself and do less damage than the potential effects of some of the music.

I know that kids have to learn to make choices about what they see and read and do, and I'm realistic enough to know that I'm not the only one to have a part in bringing up my children. But they don't have to learn by bitter experience. They start off making choices when they are very small. Our job is to inculcate in them moral values. They should be protected from bad influences until they are sufficiently mature to cope with them.

Teens can also be exposed to negative spiritual influences, with cults and gurus. This can be especially harmful because in the teen years, conversions are made. It's the age when untempered idealism reigns; when, in spite of their sophisticated talk, teens are extremely naive.

A teenager exposed to negative spiritual influence is in great danger unless he knows God and is firmly grounded in the truth. There are teens like that. But for the others, I would use whatever influence I had with the teenager and say, "I'd rather you didn't go there and these are the reasons: I believe this is a very bad spiritual influence; it is not of God, and I don't want you exposed to it." If he objects and protests, you may not be able to stop him, but at least you will have made an attempt. I believe that we will fail in many things we try to do, but our responsibility is to make the attempt and leave the results with God.

Be a Refuge in the Storm
BILL BRIGHT

OUR SOCIETY IS INFILTRATED WITH THE WORLD. SATAN IS exercising his power everyplace our children go. If there were a polio or a typhoid epidemic, we would try to protect our children from being exposed. In the same way, we must do everything we can to protect our children from the epidemic of immorality, pornography, abortion, and just plain godlessness of our society.

That's the reason I'm a strong believer in good Christian schools. Some people call them spiritual "hothouses" where students don't have to face reality. The fact is, though, that every day they are inundated with reality. They need a refuge at school, as well as at home, where they can be reminded of Christian values and God's standard of morality.

I don't think that young people need to be constantly exposed to garbage to know that garbage is bad for them. They don't have to drink in order to know the dangers of drinking, to take drugs in order to know the dangers of drugs, or to experience any of the other self-destructive behaviors common in the world in order to learn that they are harmful.

If they are not properly taught, there is a danger, however, of children turning into "hothouse Christians" unable to deal with the outside world. That's the reason I suggest that at an early age parents provide sex education, to help young people understand their bodies and appreciate the tremendous blessing that can

14

come one day as they enter into marriage without having previously experienced a sexual relationship. They need to know that sex is a beautiful thing not to be prostituted on a lonely country road in the backseat of a car, or in a drunken stupor, or on drugs. I think young people need to be told the consequences of violating the laws of God. Parents need to be very honest with their children. They need to talk openly about the human body, to discuss with their kids the reality of sex, and to point out the consequences of sex outside of marriage. Parents should also talk about what drugs do to the body and about how we become what we take into our minds and bodies. We must encourage our children to read the right literature, listen to the right music, and to avoid those things that would contaminate them—body, mind, or spirit.

If I were a parent of youngsters today, I don't think that I would allow them to watch television without guiding them in their program choices until they were in their teens. In my opinion, television is one of the major factors of the corruption of the morals of our youth. I don't think that television has anything good to offer to the average person. We've never been a television watching family. We're a reading family. I asked my older son when he was eight if he would like a television or whether he would like to have more time to read books. He said, "Oh, I'd much rather read." Our younger son, probably influenced by the example of his older brother, said, "I'd like to read too."

The Scriptures teach that we are what we think. We're all familiar with the saying, "Idle hands are the devil's workshop," so it is crucial that there be a carefully planned agenda for our children in terms of how many hours a day we spend in creative games and other activities as a family. This takes more time, energy, and forethought than simply allowing television to become a convenient baby-sitter. But what should be of greater concern to us as parents than that with which our children fill their minds? Such an investment will pay untold beneficial dividends for a lifetime.

C H A P T E R
2

How Do I
Help My Child Deal with
the Media?

Making Faith Work in a Media World
DAVID & KAREN MAINS

A HUGE SHIFT HAS TAKEN PLACE IN OUR SOCIETY. IT IS A different kind of world than the one in which we were raised. When we were children, we didn't go to movies and they had little effect on our world. But now the media, television especially, affects everything that happens.

Because the school of the world has shifted, we feel it is almost impossible to make a list of do's and don'ts for our children to follow. That's because much of what happens in our culture isn't directly spoken about in Scripture.

Of course, there are direct scriptural prohibitions, and our family is obedient to those prohibitions. But most of these ethical, moral, Christian rules are brought to bear on areas where there are no direct scriptural injunctions. The Bible doesn't say anything about television, theater, magazines, or a whole list of other things which some Christians include on their lists of do's and don'ts.

Thus, we have found that a number of the do's and don'ts that we grew up with don't help our children decide what Christian morals and ethics apply to this media-affected culture.

This creates a problem in some families because family members aren't comfortable talking about issues where faith and the lives of their children meet head-on. This results in two things: parents become dogmatic, and young people get their backs up. Those things in turn lead to continuous arguments or refusing to discuss certain subjects altogether.

This has a direct effect on the lives of many Christian teens. Some become insulated against or isolated from society. Others develop a dual standard. For instance, they think it is wrong to go to a movie but have no dilemma about watching that same movie on TV or on a video viewer. Such duplicity keeps kids from developing a critical viewing standard whereby they can measure each media piece on its own merit.

Developing a critical viewing standard is something that we've worked very hard at in our family. We've helped our children develop evaluative tools and methods whereby they apply those tools and methods to everything they see, hear, or read.

Here's how it works. First we use a rating game to get the ball rolling; then we ask questions from a Christian viewpoint about what we've rated.

Step 1: The Rating Game

If someone in our family reads a book or sees a movie, it is customary for us to say, "OK, on a scale of one to ten, what did you think of it?" (ten—high, one—low) By doing this, we are inviting the young people to share their opinions.

This helps the conversation begin without direct spiritual overtones. Instead, it begins with a personal opinion. This helps us hear where the other person is coming from, and means that we listen noncritically. We don't say such things as, "How in the world could you give that crummy thing a nine?"

We might say, "Oh, that's interesting. You gave it a six, and I gave it an eight. Why?" At that point, the children have learned to say, "Well, technically it was terrific camera work." Or, "The way the book was written was great, but I had problems with the content." They've learned to back up their ratings with a critical evaluation of what they have seen or read.

Often we make our evaluations in a family setting. For instance, coming home from church we might talk about what we thought of the sermon.

This can be fascinating because our evaluations might be radically different. For instance, since we have been Christians a long time, we might rate a sermon we've heard time after time rather low. Yet, our eleven-year-old may rate it a nine because he found tremendous value in it. What's more, it might be a topic we've never discussed with him because it was old hat to us.

When we do the evaluating, we let the kids go first. When they share things like, "I gave it a nine because it hit right where I am," we learn things about the needs of family members.

Step 2: A Christian Worldview
Once we've done this rating, we move on to the second step, asking questions that help the children come to grips with what they have seen and how it relates to their faith in God.

There are scores of questions that could be asked, including: "What was real about what you saw? What was unreal? Were there Christian themes? Anti-Christian themes?" If it was fiction, "Can you just watch it for amusement or does it say something about our world?" If sexual themes were presented, we ask questions such as: "Was the presentation honest? Do the people we know who have had affairs find the kind of happiness the film portrays? Do you know any Scriptures related to these areas?"

Let's see how this works out in our lives. Say our subscription to *Time* magazine runs out. Instead of automatically renewing, we ask every family member questions about the magazine. Thus, each person evaluates *Time* magazine's effect on his life and on his faith.

Step 3: Personal Ownership
This is a continuing process which leads our kids to a point where they have ownership of their Christian values. They are not dependent on Daddy or the church's list of do's and don'ts. They act from the base of values they themselves have developed.

To get them to this point of ownership, we generally end by asking such questions as: "How do you feel about it? Was it worth your time? Would you do it again?"

We believe that this process is part of the transformation by the renewing of the mind talked about in Romans 12:1. It makes our kids think for themselves, which makes them less dependent on peer pressure or the values promoted in the general society.

For instance, if the entire sophomore class thinks a film is great, most freshmen will immediately agree. But, Joel, our freshman son, will be able to say what he thinks of the movie and why. His ability to think critically about what he has seen will be more important than what his classmates think.

TELEVISION: MOLDER AND SHAPER OF LIVES

Most television programming is awful! According to Dr. Gerald Looney, University of Arizona, by the time the average preschool child reaches fourteen years of age, he will have witnessed 18,000 murders on TV, and countless hours of related violence, nonsense, and unadulterated drivel! Dr. Saul Kapel states, furthermore, that the most time-consuming activity in the life of a child is neither school nor family interaction. It is television, absorbing 14,000 valuable hours during the course of childhood! That is equivalent to sitting before the tube eight hours a day continuously for 4.9 years!

There are other aspects of television which demand its regulation and control. For one thing, it is an enemy of communication within the family. How can we talk to each other when a million-dollar production in living color is always beckoning our attention? I am also concerned about the current fashion whereby program directors are compelled to include all the avant-garde ideas, go a little farther, use a little more profanity, discuss the undiscussable, assault the public concept of good taste and decency. In so doing, they are hacking away at the foundations of the family and all that represents the Christian ethic. In recent seasons, for example, we were offered hilariously funny episodes about abortion, divorce, extramarital relationships, rape, and the ever-popular theme, "Father is an idiot." If this is "social relevance," then I am sick unto death of the messages I have been fed.

Television, with its unparalleled capacity for teaching and edifying, has occasionally demonstrated the potential it carries. "Little House on the Prairie" was for years the best program available for young children. I would not, therefore, recommend smashing the television set in despair. Rather, we must learn to control it instead of becoming its slave.

James Dobson

From *Dr. Dobson Answers Your Questions*, by James Dobson, Tyndale House Publishers, Inc. © 1982. Used by permission.

It's the same for our daughter, Melissa. She's a little shy, but that doesn't stop her from talking to station managers and theater managers about previews of films that were rated "G," but really aren't for general viewing. Her critical thinking gives her tremendous strength to do what she knows is right.

Our critical thinking also affects our family operations. For instance, our family has decided not to have a television set. For the past thirteen years we've lived without one. This is not something we've pushed on the kids. In fact, we've offered the kids a TV. But they have chosen not to have it. They have come to the place where they say it's an influence they would just as soon not have to contend with all the time. Instead of television, we've tried to expose the children to a wide variety of the best culture the world has to offer.

Sometimes it's hard for us to decide what to see or not to see. If that's the case, we use these guidelines: What do people whom we trust think of it? What is it rated if it is a movie? Is it the kind of thing we want to spend our time seeing or doing?

Of course, even with the best guidelines, we sometimes make mistakes. But that has a place too. It helps our kids see that there are some things that are not edifying and that they should avoid seeing in the future. It also gives us chances to discuss some of the topics that were in the show.

This happened a few summers ago when Melissa went to see a popular film while she was visiting at a friend's home. Most kids her age were going wild about the film, but when we asked

Melissa, she rated it a five and a half. She then gave us her reasons for her rating. The funny thing was that same week *Time* magazine pointed out the same flaws in the movie that Melissa had observed.

The neat thing is that this critical thinking process has helped us have a tremendous amount of trust in our children. And, in turn, they can talk about almost anything with us. For instance, the movie Melissa saw contained a sex scene. But she didn't hesitate to talk with us about it. Then we could ask such questions as: "Should you have left the theater when the scene came on? Did the scene bother you? Does it flash back into your mind?"

This process with Melissa ended with a discussion on the need to protect our minds from some of the things that non-Christians have no problem observing. That, in turn, made Melissa stronger and better able to apply her faith in Christ to her life.

And, that is the goal of this whole process: to enable our kids to critically evaluate everything they go through and to see how their faith in God applies in the different situations.

The Good and Bad of Television
TIM HANSEL

MICHAEL VANCE, A CONSULTANT WHO ONCE WORKED with Walt Disney, told participants at a seminar that television is the most important invention in human history. According to Vance, the tragedy is that the way most of us use TV, the influence is more on the negative side than the positive. "I hear people say that television is full of dumb things," Vance said. "Then I ask them what they watch, and you know what they are watching? Dumb things."

We parents need to recognize the influence TV can have on our children.

1. *Television can keep children from learning habits of perseverance, especially when it comes to problem-solving.* Our kids have been conditioned to believe that most problems can be solved in thirty minutes, and that really big problems take an

hour. That may sound comical, but at an instinctive level they really believe that. They consequently have incredible impatience when problems arise.

2. *Television can give children a distorted view of what is good, what is beautiful, and what is important.*

3. *Television can negatively affect children's self-esteem.* It does this so subtly that we don't usually recognize the process, but it's powerful nevertheless. The average viewer sees from 9,000–10,000 commericals a year. These commercials try to sell us products by convincing us that we need them. They convince us that we need them by telling us we're not OK without them. And our kids are being bombarded with these messages.

I don't think TV is necessarily bad, but we have to be aware of TV's influence, and we have to control the quality of what we watch. We don't need to break our TV sets, but we need to help our children understand what's going on. Challenge them to view television thoughtfully. Teach them to question what they see. When television gets in the way of better pursuits or higher values, turn it off and put it in the garage for a while.

Set boundaries around your children's television viewing. Limit the amount of time they can watch TV or the number of programs they can see. Direct them to programs that are informative, educational, or inspirational. Be selective—and be disciplined about staying inside the boundaries you set.

Try to control what your kids see outside the home too. We can't—and we shouldn't try to—make our kids think just the way we think, but we want to influence their thinking in the direction of Christian values. While they are still listening to us, we need to consider influences outside the home as well as within.

My kids know the difference between movies they can see and movies they can't see. The other day they had an opportunity to see an R-rated movie at a friend's house. Everyone else was saying, "Yeah, let's watch it; it'll be great." But my sons said, "No, we're not supposed to do that." They made a choice based on our family's values, and I was really proud of them.

It is important not to focus too much on television—either its good points or its bad. After all, even the best TV shows aren't good enough to be at the center of our lives. I want my kids to feel that life is too wonderful to miss out on by spending it in front of the television set.

Television Affects Your Children Even When It's Off
ANTHONY CAMPOLO

IN OUR AGE, TELEVISION IS MORE RESPONSIBLE FOR DETER-mining what children become than perhaps any other single factor. It provides role models, people for children to pattern their lives after. It affects peer relationships and sets standards of group behavior. In addition, it gives children a view of reality that affects all areas of their childhood.

Television provides role models. In their play, children tend to imitate characters on television shows. Since play is the major instrument of learning for children, anything that affects play is crucial to their development in all areas. If they imitate good role models, their development will be enhanced; if they imitate bad role models, it will be harmed.

What kinds of role models do they find on the TV screen? It has been said that ours is the age of celebrity. The difference between celebrities and heroes is that heroes are people who do awesome and fantastic things; celebrities are simply people who are prominent, whether good, bad, or mediocre. The TV celebrities that children imitate are often far from being heroes.

I am very frightened, as most of us are, at the rise of rock videos. A whole new set of models is being presented not only to teenagers but to children as well. The MTV channel specializes in rock videos that give very explicit information about sadomasochism and degradation of women. The styles of dress and of singing all are aimed at hating what is healthy and good about society. Even the strongest defenders of rock music would have to admit that satanism is an overt and explicit theme of significant proportion.

Of less dramatic, but greater significance is the glorification of questionable living arrangements, such as situation comedies in which men and women live together, in which the divorced lifestyle is made more attractive than the married lifestyle, and in which homosexuality is made to appear normal.

Television affects peer relationships. Any school, Christian or public, is made up of a variety of subcultural groups. These groups take on the values they have picked up in the media. We used to think the peer group was a value-creating entity, and a person's values changed as he changed peer groups. That's not true. Nowadays the peer group does not create values; it simply adopts the values created by television. What groups wear, how they talk, what they think is right and wrong—these factors are all influenced by television. The peer group becomes a reinforcer of TV values.

Grade-school children are less prone to adopting peer-reinforced TV values than are teenagers because small children are influenced more by their teachers than by their peer group. But even small children have problems—many schoolteachers are media creations. Their teaching methods and the values they transmit are strongly influenced by television.

Television gives children an ugly view of reality. Television is doing away with the concept of childhood. Childhood should be a time of playing, growing, and learning in the security of the home. Children need not know everything about the world. We should conceal from them certain violent realities. We should protect them from certain ugly dimensions of human existence. Children should learn about life little by little, so that by the late teen years they understand what it means to live in our kind of world.

But it is one of the horrible realities of our time that children don't have a childhood anymore. Just a generation ago children could feel secure because the major form of communication was reading, and the ugly things were seldom put in children's books. Now television has intruded, and many children have lost the possibility of a warm, trusting, secure childhood.

It is interesting to note that there is a trend toward stark realism in literature for children and young people. Since the decade of the '70s, many books are being published that offer a slice of life—descriptive stories without happy endings or even satisfactory resolutions in which there are problems with no solutions, suffering without respite or hope, and a cast of characters without heroes or heroines. Children's literature is beginning to imitate television in order to compete.

Fortunately, there are still books that challenge the minds and elevate the spirits of children, but the trend toward stark realism is strong and harks back to the beginning of the century when children's stories were cautionary tales designed to warn about danger or to frighten them into good behavior. But these stories, like folk tales, had an aura of fantasy about them that softened their impact and made them entertaining. Today's realistic stories offer life without a fairy godmother.

What is ugly about television is not the make-believe shows. Children are able to differentiate between reality and make-believe. The real problem lies in the "reality shows"—talk shows, specials, and news broadcasts that conceal nothing from children. By the time the average individual is nine years old, his childhood—his secure, problem-free growing time—is over. By age nine, the child knows about homosexuality and child pornography, murder, and war. He has learned to suspect everyone.

Television indeed affects our children. It bombards them with celebrities who often lack moral values but who do exciting things, and our children imitate them. It determines the standards of the various groups found in any school or neighborhood, and our children, in their natural desire to belong, pick up these values in order to be accepted. It exposes our children to all kinds of evil that erodes the secure world they should be able to experience during their early years. What can parents do to counteract the potentially deadly effects of TV?

First, parents must use judgment as to how much and what their children watch. Perhaps they could confine the set to the parents' bedroom and permit the children to watch only certain programs at certain times. By using wisdom and common sense, parents can shield their children from both damaging role models and ugly realities.

Second, parents can steer their children toward helpful programs. It's a good idea for very small children to become "Mister Rogers" fans, for example. Mr. Rogers is a Christian, and he knows about and understands children. On his program he introduces play styles that communicate Christian values and that help the child become kinder and more sensitive.

Third, parents should be aware of potentially damaging influences at school. If parents see their children being socialized by teachers whose value systems are anti-Christian, they should pull the children out of the school and get them into a private school or teach them at home.

Fourth, parents should consider the possibility of removing television from the household completely, especially during the early years of child rearing. If they decide to keep a television, they must be able to control it. If control is too difficult for them, getting rid of the set is the only answer. It may seem like a hard price to pay, but it could make a tremendous difference to the children's futures.

If getting rid of TV is the only way out, then do it. It's not too huge a sacrifice to make when you consider that your children's futures may be at stake.

Your Children and the Movies
DAVID & GAIL VEERMAN

IN THE CHURCH OF MY YOUTH, MOVIES WERE BANNED. Not that we didn't have films *in* church, but good church members were expected to avoid theaters where Hollywood's profits were made. Most of the movies, we were told, were blatantly sinful, and even the "good" films gathered money to support the depraved lifestyles of those in the movie industry.

While these unilateral prohibitions may have been an overreaction (and even counterproductive in the lives of curious teenagers), they contained much truth. From Hollywood has flowed a steady celluloid stream of non-Christian and even anti-Christian values and morals.

But now we live in the "enlightened '80s" where evangelicals can frequent the theater of their choice without even a twinge of guilt. How ironic—our freedoms have increased while movies have become even greater purveyors of immorality.

In both eras, however, the real issue is not the theater or even the film. As with music, books, magazines, television, and other entertainment media, movies are not evil in themselves. It is what they portray and how they are used that make the difference. The easy response is to ban them, trying to shield our children from their terrible effects. But this is not the best way. Instead, we must teach our kids how to choose and how to watch. This is especially important in this age when cable, satellite dishes, video stores, and "Watchmans" invade every corner of our lives. The moral pressures and choices on our children are much greater than when we were their age.

Given this somewhat philosophical backdrop, what should be our *practical* response? How do we select the movies that our children can see and how do we teach them in the midst of this process?

1. *Decide beforehand what you want your children to see relative to their age- and maturity-levels.* Talk this over with your spouse and determine your guidelines as responsible Christian parents. Don't wait to be surprised by the question, "Can I go with So-and-so to see Such-and-such?" (to which many parents answer, "I don't know; go ask your mother/father.") These guidelines and ground rules could include who makes the film (e.g., Disney), its rating, and other factors. Obviously, you can't be too specific, but it is important to come to a general understanding *before* the situation arises.

2. *Learn as much as you can about the movie.* The rating system will be helpful, but *do not* rely on it exclusively. My experience has been that "G" films are safe, but after that the system gets shaky (and this could change in the future). *Talk to other parents* about the movie; but make sure these are parents whom you trust, sharing your values and outlook. Other parents may think a movie is fine when you would think the same one is terrible.

Consider the reviews of the movie that you hear or read, especially those in Christian magazines. *Campus Life, Christianity Today, Group,* and others have movie reviews as a regular feature. Of course, these will be geared to high-school age and older, but their comments will be helpful.

3. *Go with them.* Though the *Care Bears* movie won't be very entertaining for you, just being with your child will help build your relationship. For other movies which are not so obviously "safe," you will be able to see for yourself the content and influence to which your child is being subjected. This will give you something to discuss and insight to pass on to other concerned parents.

Of course, it won't always be possible or practical for you to accompany your child to the show. In these situations, however, it is important to make sure that they are well-chaperoned and safe. Younger children (until about age nine) should *always* be with an adult or an older teenager. The friend's parent or older brother or sister would be all right *if you know and trust them.* Whatever you do, don't just drop them off at the theater with instructions concerning what to see and where and when you will pick them up. Don't use movies as baby-sitters.

If your older child (nine and above) will not be with an adult, make sure that he or she goes with another child or group. Don't send a child alone. Unfortunately, these last two precautions are necessary because of the kind of society in which we live where child-stealing has become commonplace. This is also important because most theaters have multiple auditoriums where the whole range of ratings are featured. The lobby will be filled with all ages and types of people. And some theaters are very lax about who goes into which movie. In other words, it would be very possible for a child to wander in (on purpose or by accident) to a "PG-13" or "R" movie.

4. *Be a good example.* There will be times when you attend movies that are off limits to your children. When this happens, be sure to let them know why they are all right for you and your reasons for attending those specific films. They should see that your life is guided by the thoughtful application of scriptural principles.

5. *Tell them why.* Don't just say they can't go to a certain movie—share your reasons. Explain that there are certain scenes, ideas, or subject matter that are not appropriate for them, and tell why. They may not agree (after all, *their friends* saw the movie), but at least they will know that you have thought it through. This would be the time to share the importance of the principle of Philippians 4:8—that we should fix our thoughts on what is good and helpful, not on evil and "trash."

6. *Watch for opportunities to teach.* The mistake of many Christian adults is thinking that the most dangerous aspects of movies are scenes on the screen—explicit sex, violence, and language. These definitely are problems. But what can be more devastating are the subtle messages portrayed by lifestyles and philosophies. Usually these are not covered by the rating system, and they can be found even in children's films. A few messages of which you should be aware are:

● Pleasure is most important.

- Money solves any problem.
- Success equals fame, power, fortune.
- Religious people are eccentric or unusual.
- Life is cheap and death is "clean."
- Love conquers all.
- Life's problems can be solved without God.

Even the Disney "classics" carry ideas of romanticized love, racial and regional stereotypes, and materialism.

Teaching, however, should not be limited to discussing the negative aspects of the movie. Drama can be a powerful way to portray truth. Poverty, war, broken families, and other struggles are often graphically pictured, as are friendship, love, service, and other positive qualities. These themes will also make good discussion starters.

Whatever message the movie gives—an illicit sexual innuendo, a curse word, wanton violence, subtle worldliness, or a positive concept or theme—it can be an opportunity to teach your child about life, the Christian faith, how to apply faith to life, and how to "read" the movies.

Being a parent is not easy in this age of "freedom" and openness—there are continual, daily decisions to make and enforce. Through all of the choosing, screening, and disciplining, our goal must be to help our children mature and grow. We want them to be able to learn to make their own responsible decisions after we are out of the picture. Use movies to teach.

What About Rock Music?
DAVID & GAIL VEERMAN

A FEW MONTHS AGO OUR YOUNGEST DAUGHTER ANnounced that she really liked Madonna (the rock singer whose questionable lifestyle and song lyrics have vaulted her to stardom). After recovering from the initial shock, we began to share with her just a bit about how that probably was not a good idea. Later, Gail and I talked about how difficult it is to shield kids from all the wrong influences. We don't play "Madonna-music" in the house or car, but our six-year-old had heard the songs . . . and liked them. Of course, she had no idea what the words meant—she just liked the songs that her friends were singing or playing.

Rock music presents a number of problems for the Christian parent. The lyrics can be vile, with themes ranging from sex to suicide, from drugs to death. And even when the words seem innocent, the video version will often feature violence and perversion.

Another problem with rock music is its "stars." Many of them openly advocate and practice sexual promiscuity and perversion, drug usage, and other anti-Christian, antisocial lifestyles. In popular music these days it seems that the more outrageous you are, the more records you sell. These are not the heroes we want for our children.

When parents see and hear these rock performers, they are tempted to burn the albums, smash the tapes, and banish the beat from the house . . . forever. Though that response is easy to understand, it really won't solve the problem. (And, it may even prove counterproductive, piquing the child's curiosity about these banned musicians or pushing them toward rebellion.)

VIDEOS

"When we bought our VCR, I thought that we would have more control over our family's entertainment. But now that everyone has them, and a lot of tapes, I think we have less control. There's no telling what my kids watch at their friends' homes."

Have you ever said or thought those words? It isn't easy to monitor our children's viewing habits in this video age. The VCR can be a valuable tool for a family, allowing us to bring into the home positive, healthy family entertainment in place of the usual television fare. And there are scores of excellent Christian tapes available, from classes to concerts. But other families have different values and rules, and the movie banned in your home may be owned and played at a friend's.

This problem cannot be totally eliminated, but these steps will help:

1. *Talk through your "evaluation grid" with your children.* In other words, let them know why you don't like certain films, why others are totally off limits, etc. Help them understand how to make choices in light of your family's Christian values. And encourage them to talk to you if they have questions.

2. *Be willing to say no to your kids.* For many parents, this is difficult, but it is necessary.

3. *Don't come down so hard on the children that you encourage them to lie.* In other words, how you respond to a "violation" is very important. The idea is to keep the communication lines open. Remember, it isn't easy for a child to say no to his peers (and the peers' parents).

4. *Talk with them* after *the fact too.* Look for the teachable moment. You could ask what they were feeling as they watched the movie and whether they think the movie is a good or bad influence on kids.

5. *Talk with the friend's parents.* It is unreasonable to expect your child to bear all the pressure of saying no, especially when the other parents are renting and showing tapes which they have selected. If there is a repeated problem in certain homes, get with the other folks. Let them know how you feel and explain your family guidelines. When you do this, be sure not to have a judgmental attitude.

Be prepared and communicate. Help videos become "blessings," not "curses."

YFC Editors

In reality, music itself is neither good nor bad. There is nothing inherently sinful about a certain beat or chord progression. What makes the moral difference is how it is used—this is where the performer, listener, and lyrics enter the picture. To ban a certain style of music, therefore, would be wrong. Throughout history most musical forms have been labeled "sinful" at one time or another—everything from Mozart and Bach to big bands, jazz, and hard rock. Instead of rejecting a musical style, we should view music as we would any other "neutral" object.

Here are a few suggestions for teaching children how to make positive and healthy musical choices:

1. *Be aware of what is out there.* Before you can talk intelligently about popular music, you will have to have to have some idea of who the performers are, what they are like, and what they are singing and saying. You don't have to be a constant listener of "top 40" radio to learn. Listen occasionally and pick up a list of the hit songs at a record store. There are also magazines which print the words to all the top songs. One of these would be helpful. (You could even sneak an occasional peek at MTV.) There are Christian resources as well. Each month, *Campus Life* magazine reviews top secular and Christian artists. This is a very valuable tool.

2. *Be a good example.* If you want to teach your children to have balanced musical tastes, listen to a variety of music. Make it a family project to educate each other about each person's favorite type of music. And explore new music together. Go to an opera; rent a tape of a Broadway musical; play gospel and soul on the radio; and watch for opportunities to experience ballet, folk, and jazz. (Usually public television offers a good variety.) If you can appreciate different types of music, your children will learn to do the same. And let them know why you like a certain song.

3. *Inform them of alternatives.* There are many *good* musicians in popular music who project a positive image and sing meaningful, poignant, and helpful songs. Let your children know about these men and women. And, of course, there is the growing field of Christian performers. Today's Christian music is of highest quality and features a variety of styles and sounds. Don't limit their listening to Christian artists, but be sure to play the music and add the records to your library. The words will be Christ-centered; but, just as important, these young men and women offer healthy role models.

4. *Teach discernment.* Without over-reacting or preaching, let your children know how you feel about certain lyrics and specific performers. Teach them to ask the right questions about their entertainment choices. These include:
- What is the song's message?
- What does this song do for me? My thoughts? My feelings? My actions?

- What kind of person is the performer?
- Is listening to this "honoring Christ"?

When the opportunities arise, talk about the positives and negatives of rock lyrics you have heard. Most of the time our younger children have no idea of the lifestyles of the stars or the real meaning of the words. Our older daughter (ten at the time) was "grossed out" when we told her of some of the platform antics of a certain performer, and she decided to stop listening to his music.

5. *Be ready to compromise.* If we really want our children to learn to decide for themselves as they grow and mature, we must give them opportunities to make decisions. Therefore, negotiation will often be necessary in "no-win" situations. Compromise; make deals; make concessions—always with a good-natured, positive attitude, with the goal of helping them learn to make the right choices themselves. For example, allow the stereo to be played (at their desired volume) during a certain time period, or offer to "put up with" their music if they "put up with" yours, or rent a music video of their favorite song or artist, watch it together, and discuss it afterward.

Rock music can be a powerful influence in our children's lives—we dare not ignore it or ban it. Instead, we must seize the initiative and teach them how to choose, how to listen, and help them build good and thoughtful listening habits. It is very important during these early years to teach (and learn with) our children. Later, as peer pressure intensifies, the bad habits will be hard to break.

C H A P T E R
3

How Do I
Help My Child Deal with
Sex and Dating?

Feeling Comfortable about Sex
GRACE KETTERMAN, M.D.

BEFORE AGE SIX, CHILDREN WANT TO KNOW WHY THEY are physically different from the opposite sex. They also are curious about where babies come from and how the baby gets into Mommy. They ask questions like, "Could I have a baby?" and "How might a baby get in my tummy?"

Older children may be curious about the size of their father's genitals or their mother's breasts if they happen to see their parents nude. Through the media, children are becoming aware of a variety of sexual behaviors, and they may ask questions about homosexuality or unmarried adults who live together.

As children develop sexually, they need to understand what is happening to their bodies. Girls in particular are developing early, with some nine- and many ten-year-old girls menstruating.

Most children have many questions but are reluctant to ask them because their parents are awkward talking about sex. The key to talking about sex is being comfortable with your own sexuality. If you see sex as a wholesome and good part of God's creation, it will be easier to talk with your children about it. It helps to talk with trusted friends about sexual matters in a wholesome way. The more you talk about sex (within sensible limits), the more confident, knowledgeable, and comfortable you will be when you talk about it with your children.

1. *Start early.* Children begin to learn the facts of life by the way we handle their bodies. We can start promoting healthy sexuality by caring for the boy's circumcision and the girl's genital area in a gentle and straightforward way. When we screw up our faces and turn up our noses at the smell of a dirty diaper, the baby will pick up the attitude that this is a dirty, ugly part of the body. We need to communicate that God made the whole body lovely—our hands, our faces, and our genitals. By our actions and attitudes we can teach our children that their entire bodies are beautiful creations of God.

It's normal for children to explore their bodies; we should accept this as a healthy way for them to find out about themselves. When babies start exploring their bodies, we can help them identify the nose, the ears, the eyes, and also the genitals. I did this with my infant grandson. When he would touch his little penis and have an erection, I would gently say, "Andy, that's your penis, and it feels good and that's fine." If I had slapped his hand and said, "That's terrible, don't touch," he would have subconsciously remembered that part of his body was not good.

2. *Share the responsibility.* Both parents should talk to their children about sex, rather than only the mother with the daughters and the father with the sons. Each one adds a special perspective. After a mother gives her response she can say, "Why don't you go talk to Daddy about this, because he can tell you how men feel. I can only tell you how women feel."

3. *Answer simply.* We need to stop and think about what the child is really asking. If a child asks about babies, don't explain menstruation. When we get nervous we either talk too much or talk in a way that tells the child we are anxious. So give a simple, direct answer to the question, and then give an invitation for more questions—"Does that explain it?" or "Is that OK?" or "If you want to know more, be sure to ask me." That way, the child always has a gateway for further questions.

A parent may say too much as a subconscious way of shutting off further discussion, thinking, "If I tell my child everything now, he won't bother me anymore." The child will be bored with the long, detailed explanation and won't ask the parents again. We need to share in such a way that our children will feel free to come back again and ask us more.

4. *Use teachable moments.* Often children ask questions because of something they have seen in the media or heard about at school. This may include rape, homosexuality, or abortion. When my daughter was nine, she asked me what rape is. Instead of shielding her from the truth, I explained what it is and said, "Men do wrong things like that when they don't love God and don't know how to live by His rules. We need to pray for God to help them learn how to be better people." I didn't want her to feel condemning toward rapists but compassionate. But I wanted her to realize the difference between people who love God and people who reject Him.

If a young child comes home confused or shocked at what she saw or heard at school, we can say, "Those children are getting into behaviors that are for adults when they should be playing ball and having fun. You don't have to worry about those things now, but I want you to know a little more about them." Then we can explain simply and ask her if she has any questions.

5. *Counter the influence of the media.* It's important for us to watch television programs with small children and point out what we think about them. After children turn eight this is not as helpful because then they start to be less interested in our ideas. But small children are very willing to hear what we believe about the situations presented on television. We can give them a few scenarios television does not give. For example, if an unmarried couple is living together on television, we could point out that rather than living happily ever after, one of them might abruptly leave. Giving children the less glamorous outcomes will help them see beyond what the media shows.

6. *Initiate discussions.* If children never ask about sexuality, either because they are not interested or because they have been frightened, we should not ignore the subject. By the time a child is nine, we need to say, "Honey, I've noticed you've never asked me about babies or about sexual matters. Maybe we could talk about it."

Whatever the age our children express an interest in learning about sexuality, we cannot afford to shut them off. Later they may not be so open to learning God's perspective on sexuality.

Discussing Sex with Teenagers
RONALD HUTCHCRAFT

THE *FIRST* OF FOUR ESSENTIAL STEPS WHEN DISCUSSING sex is to give teens the correct information. Call intercourse "intercourse." Call the parts of the body by their right names. Don't be too cute; teens don't appreciate halfway answers to their questions. They know that babies are not left by storks.

Second, give them co-ed information. By that I mean that both Mom and Dad need to be involved in educating teens about sex. I am convinced that no woman fully understands male sexuality, and no man has a complete understanding of female sexuality.

For example, a man is the best person to explain to a daughter how men are stimulated more by sight than by touch. A mother can explain this but, because she hasn't actually experienced male sexuality, she can only convey what someone else has told her. Likewise, a mother is the best person to explain to her son about how a woman is stimulated more by touch than by sight.

A father can't explain this as well. Neither can he do as meaningful a job telling how a woman looks for leadership qualities in a man and how she would rather have a moral leader than someone who wants to play a cat-and-mouse game of "How far does he want me to go tonight?"

Third, take the initiative to talk about sex more than just once in a while, and let teens know you're comfortable with the subject. Try to get away from the idea of one or two "big talks." I've learned to bring the subject up as often as is comfortable, and recently I saw the value in that.

One day my son said to me, "Dad, when are we going to have *the* talk? You know, the one about sex and stuff." So we started to talk, and in a few minutes he said, "Oh, is that all?" "Yes," I said, "we've been having this talk all along."

TALK ABOUT SEX EARLY

A lot of times communication breaks down in the teen years because parents do not understand the teen world. It is easy to think we have always been as mature as we are now. We forget our own struggles. But no matter where we grew up, we were not faced with the choices about drugs and sex that our kids today have to make at an early age.

With our parents, it was normal for a girl to reach puberty at about age thirteen to fifteen, sometimes as late as sixteen or seventeen. Now it is not uncommon to find girls who are nine or ten starting their first menstrual cycle. Kids have so few years to get ready for this new sexual identity, and it consequently puts more stress on their teen years. Yet, though there is more sexual freedom, we are no better prepared to handle it.

Instead of being uptight about sex, we as parents need to be aware of our permissive culture and our children's premature adolescence, and consider what practical steps we can take to keep ahead of the times. For one, we can talk about sex with our children much earlier than we think it needs to be discussed.

Jim & Sally Conway

One of the best ways to take the initiative in talking to your teens about sex is to bring up your courtship. Kids like to hear about it, and you can tell it to them with both humor and seriousness. Another way is to tell them about certain television programs that you're not going to watch. Why aren't you going to watch them? Then talk to your teens about some of the sexual values communicated by those programs. Or, one other way is to ask your kids what their friends are saying about certain subjects. The point is, it's up to you—the parents—to initiate these talks; you have to locate and isolate the teachable moments.

Fourth, it is your responsibility to create a model of healthy sexuality. If my wife and I are consistently telling our teens to wait for marriage before having sex, then we'd better show them a marriage that's worth waiting for. If they don't see Mom and Dad affectionately touching and hugging each other, then the marriage looks boring and dull. Obviously, you don't want to show them moments of deep intimacy, but there is nothing wrong with displaying kisses and hugs of affection.

When our youngest son was a baby sitting in his high chair, Karen and I would be hugging and soon we'd hear him banging his cereal bowl on the tray. We would quickly turn around to see little Brad watching us, clapping his hands, and laughing. It was an infant's appreciation of his mom's and dad's affection for each other; in his own way he was telling us to go for it.

Another parental responsibility—and certainly the most important—is to communicate God's standards on sex. God made sex something special; keep it special. His requirement of sex only in marriage is a pathway to sex at its best.

Be positive yet realistic. Don't be embarrassed to tell your teens that God invented sex, its beauty, and pleasure when it is tied to the bonds of total marital commitment. "Rejoice with the wife of your youth . . . be thou ravished always with her love" (Prov. 5:18-19, KJV). That's pretty explicit, but that's the Inventor talking.

God says, when you're married, go for it. But save it for that one special man or woman He has saved for you. Keep sex special, and you will have sex at its best. Don't settle for anything less by taking sex out of marriage.

Stress to teens that when God created sex, He put a fence around it called marriage. When you take sex outside the fence, people end up hurt and lonely. For a couple in marriage, sex brings them closer together; for a couple outside of marriage, sex drives them farther apart. When they break up, it's like ripping their hearts out because people weren't made to break up with the person they have sex with. Sex was designed for two people in a forever commitment. When sex is not treated this way, it's like tearing apart two pieces of paper which have been glued together.

God's standard is not only right, it's smart; there's something in it for us.

Helping Your Teen through
the Dating Game
JOSH McDOWELL

BY THE TIME TEENAGERS BEGIN DATING, MUCH OF THE preparation their parents can give them has already been done. Their attitudes toward the opposite sex began forming when they were in the cradle. The way their father treats their mother—the respect, admiration, and love he shows for her—becomes a model for good relationships with the opposite sex. If

CAN YOU TRUST YOUR TEEN ON A DATE?

The biblical perspective on sex is a minority view today in our society. The average American teenager has probably watched 15,000 to 20,000 hours of TV, which means he or she has stored up a lot of unbiblical input. Add to that the pressure exerted by other kids, and you have some of the reasons why a majority of adolescents—even Christian ones—are most likely sexually active.

As the child grows, you can help him or her to understand in stages what sex is all about. You can explain what Scripture says about sex, and help the young person to develop a sound standard of sexual expression. You can let him or her know how others will try to use pressure to bend that standard.

Beyond that, however, all you can do is trust your teen and pray. Your trust may be broken. But as Christian parents, you can offer real help if and when the teen slips up and falls into sin. You can help your adolescent to realize that forgiveness is available through Christ, and that his life can go on from there.

Norman Wright

the parents get angry with each other or take each other for granted, that also is a model for the children. That is why it is important that they see their parents apologize to each other and ask forgiveness.

THE COST OF DATING

Without blinking, a teen can spend a hundred dollars or more on a date. Concert tickets, dinners, transportation, and other miscellaneous expenses add up quickly.

As parents, we should be concerned about what our kids do on their dates and how much is spent. At the same time, however, we want to trust them and move them toward independence.

Communication is the key. Hopefully, we will have a strong enough relationship with our teenagers to be able to discuss dating openly and honestly. We should let them know that they have freedom to design their dates and that they have our trust. (Of course, we always will have the right to "veto.") But we should also encourage them to be *creative* in dating. The best dates are not necessarily the most expensive (contrary to popular opinion), and many inexpensive or free activities offer great opportunities for fun and getting to know the other person. These could include hiking, tennis, community service, parlor games, zoo visits, parades, "fast food" or "specialty" progressive dinners, scavenger or treasure hunts, ball games, Frisbee tossing, wading, fishing, and a myriad of other activities.

Dating, like automobile use and other expenses, should be a part of the teen's budget—we should encourage this and teach through it.

YFC Editors

Being a good role model is the most effective way to prepare children for dating, but what parents say is also important. Even small children notice the way their father talks about women, for example. And children need information about dating that is best given by the parents. Rules and guidelines are important because teenagers do not have the experience to know how to act in all

DATING AND SELF-ESTEEM

As your teen enters his dating years, try to be aware of his thoughts. It is normal for teenagers to be insecure during this time and to have a low degree of self-esteem.

Help point out that God places a much higher value on him than he puts on himself. The accompanying chart is to help you begin to understand what your teen might be going through on the inside, and what you can say to help build self-confidence.

What Your Teen Thinks	What God Thinks
(If your teen is dating): How does dating this person make me look in the eyes of other people?	Have you considered how I feel about your dating this person?
What do I *want* to do? How will this date affect me?	What *should* you do? How will this date affect the other person and your relationship with Me?
(If your teen is not yet dating): I'm a nobody unless I'm dating someone.	Your self-worth should be based on how *I* feel about you—not someone else.
My life is being wasted.	Use this time to become a godly person.
I need to work harder to get dates.	You need to work harder to to become the person I want you to be.

Barry St. Clair

situations. Education is passing on experiences and knowledge so another person doesn't have to make the same mistakes you did.

One general guideline I would give my children is to be careful not to arouse the sexual feelings and emotions of their dates. Kids need to watch where they go and what they do there. If a couple watches a sexually explicit R-rated movie from the back seat of a car in a drive-in theater, only supernatural intervention could keep their sexual feelings under control.

Another general guideline is always to treat the other person with respect. I'd tell my son to treat his date the way he would want his friends to treat his sister. An important guideline for all human relations, not just dating, is to pay attention to the other person's enjoyment.

In addition to general guidelines, parents should make some specific dating rules. A boy, when he picks up his date, should ask her parents what time she should be home. If for some reason he cannot make the curfew, he should call her parents. He owes them that much; he is taking out a precious part of their family.

For the most part, single dating should not begin until the junior or senior year of high school. Group dating or double dating may be OK earlier than that, depending on the young person's emotional maturity and spiritual insight. A person shouldn't date until he or she is able to say no, for instance, to sexual advances. A young person's level of maturity has a lot to do with the kind of relationship he has with his parents. If there is a lot of love at home, a lot of hugging and kissing, children usually won't seek that abroad. Teenagers are much better equipped to control their emotions when they are with other teenagers if they can let their emotions out at home.

I would advise my children not to kiss on the first date. A kiss is something meaningful, an expression of intimacy, a communication of deep feeling. Most people do not have that intimacy after only one date. I wouldn't try to turn my good advice into a dating rule, however. That wouldn't do any good.

Sometimes a teenager gets too deeply involved with a boyfriend or girlfriend. It helps if the parents already have a strong relationship with the teen. They then may be able to get him or her to talk the situation through with them.

Parents may have to put down some pretty strict guidelines

43

about seeing the boyfriend or girlfriend. A friend of mine did just that. He sat down with his tenth-grade daughter and said, "I think that right now you should be nothing more than friends. It has gone a little too far." The girl later told me that she backed off from the relationship with her boyfriend because she had such deep respect for her family.

It's good for teenagers to date. The purpose of dating is not only to select a mate; it's also to have fun, and to learn to feel comfortable around people of the opposite sex. Still, some teens aren't interested in dating, and parents should not force them or even encourage them too strongly. Anytime you try to force a teenager to do anything, you're going to get reaction—rebellion. Kids have to set their own pace.

Some teens have the opposite problem. They want to date, but nobody wants to go out with them. The mother and father should talk together about what may be keeping the child from dating. Does she turn people off? Is he obnoxious or unfriendly? Does she dress or wear her hair in a way that is unacceptable to the other kids? If the parents find one or two problems that can be corrected, they can then concentrate on helping the teen overcome these. Parents don't need to tell the child why they are trying to help; telling him could make him too self-conscious to make the improvements.

Some teens are better looking than others. Some are not good-looking at all. But even if people are really ugly according to the accepted standards of beauty, they will still be invited out if they develop a healthy self-esteem, show an interest in other people, and are fun to be around. Parents who pressure their teen to do something about his or her appearance may end up accentuating the problem. The teen develops a negative attitude and is no longer fun to be around.

Unattractive people can improve their appearance by the way they dress or do their hair, but more important is their ability to relate to other people. When I directed Campus Crusade on one campus, I met a girl who was unattractive and obese but very popular. Everyone wanted her at their parties because she was so much fun. She was friendly and interested in what others were doing, and people just wanted to be around her. Good looks don't last long, but children who are self-assured and interested in others have an asset that will last a lifetime.

When Are Teens Ready to Date?
BARRY ST. CLAIR

A PROBLEM FACED BY MOST PARENTS IS DECIDING WHEN their child is old enough (or mature enough) to begin dating. When that time comes for you, I think the first thing you should do is sit down with your child and define some specific dating standards. (These should be worked through together. If you try to dictate your standards to your child without his input, they will only be wasted words to him.)

The next step is helping your child determine to follow those dating standards in the future, no matter what it might cost him. Emphasize that his desire (or lack of desire) to follow his predetermined dating standards will affect four areas of his life:

- His worship of God (Isa. 59:1-2)
- His self-image (Ps. 16:1-11)
- His witness to others around him (1 Peter 3:15-16)
- His wedding (Song 2:16)

Teach your teen that if he discovers the importance of established dating standards and puts them into practice while he is young, he will see long-range positive effects in his life. Otherwise, he will see long-range negative effects. As the old saying goes, "You reap what you sow. You reap more than you sow. You reap later than you sow."

When setting dating standards, he should ask questions like:
- How old should I be?
- What do I want my dating relationships to be like?
- What qualities do I want to see in the person I date?
- How will I treat my dates?

After your teen writes down questions from every possible area of dating life that he can think of, use the Bible to discover God's answers to those questions. Make sure the standards are specific. And after your teen decides in his heart that he will not compromise those standards, have him show them to his dates when he begins to go out.

Perhaps all these steps seem like a lot to go through just to begin dating. But remember at all times—and make sure your child understands this—that our goal is to please God and not

45

ourselves. When a teen can glorify God in his dating relationships, the other areas of his life are likely to shape up as well.

CHAPTER 4

How Do I Help My Child Deal with Money?

Kids Want Everything!
LARRY RICHARDS

I NEVER WALK THROUGH A STORE, IT SEEMS, WITHOUT MY children pointing to items and trying in one way or another to get them. Children want everything they see. And why not? Television constantly bombards them with visual images of new and more exciting toys.

We adults fall into the same trap—we want new clothes, cars, and "toys" when advertisements entice us to believe we really *need* them. Why shouldn't our children, who receive the same input, have the same desires?

The first step in the process of keeping our children away from constantly *wanting* is for us parents to make some value decisions and then discipline ourselves against our own desires. As we give in to ourselves, we give in to our children; as we discipline ourselves, our children also will learn restraint. If we're going to train our children, we parents have to make some decisions ourselves.

Then we need to decide the number and kinds of toys we are going to permit our children to have. Cluttering children's lives with toys gives them a false sense of being able to have anything they want. I notice an unbelievable amount of toys in some people's homes, hundreds of dollars worth of obstacle course that the kids don't care whether they have or not. This reveals distorted values on the parents' part.

Parents need to set up some criteria for purchases. Toys should not be so small that they're going to get lost easily. They should not be so flimsy that they fall apart. Toys should stimulate creative play and have a variety of uses. Children are like little sponges; they soak up any learning opportunities around them. Don't stifle all their potential with too many toys or constant exposure to toys, like TV, that require no mind or motor stimulation.

A toy should not be purchased in order to get the child to quit whining about how much he wants it. That only lays the groundwork for constant whining because he will always want something new.

One method I've found very effective in keeping my children from thinking they must have everything they see is the allowance. If children own and control their own money, when one says, "I want this," the parent can respond, "That will cost you two weeks' allowance." Suddenly the value of the item changes; it takes on a whole different perspective. Children's attitudes change rapidly when it's their own money, rather than Mom's and Dad's, that's being spent.

When my oldest son started getting an allowance, he used it to buy junk—candy, cheap toys. After noticing this pattern, I decided to help him think about value. I sat down with him and asked him what had happened to the things he bought with his allowance. Of course, he didn't have them anymore. We talked about some things he could buy that would be more lasting, things he wanted; and we set up a savings program. If he could save up half the amount needed to buy the item, then we would provide the rest.

As the child begins to see that he needs to make responsible choices as to how he spends his money, he begins to set a lifelong pattern for saving and spending.

Different people in our society have different amounts of mon-

RAISING KIDS ON A LIMITED INCOME

When raising children on a limited income, you must constantly focus on your values. Are you scrambling to give your kids everything you never had? Are you trying to show your neighbors you're an excellent provider? Do you feel guilty because you can't give your kids the best? Then your values are off base. Worst of all, you're teaching your children to expect handouts.

Having a limited income is not a crime. You can teach your children true values—including the value of money—by how you use what you have and how you act toward it. You must carve out your values and priorities, not by comparing yourself with your neighbor, but by trusting God to provide and asking Him to help you use wisely the resources He gives.

Dick Hagstrom

ey available for discretionary use. Some don't have much; some have more than they know what to do with. I have one good friend who bought his children jumping horses. Well, I couldn't spend $30,000 on a jumping horse if I wanted to, but to him it wasn't that much money. This same man, however, brought up his kids to learn the value of money. One daughter had to take care of a goat, milk it, and sell the milk. His purpose wasn't simple lifestyle; it was to teach the child that she had to make some responsible choices with what she owned. That's the key to good money management.

Children, just like their parents, are always going to want more and better things. We parents need first to discipline ourselves against the bombardment that makes us feel we must have certain things to keep us happy. If we do that, we are far better armed to help our children learn that they just can't have everything they want—few people ever do. And by learning this lesson ourselves, we'll be far better examples to our children.

We can also help our children by teaching them that they

must care for the toys they already have so that they last. When we do get toys for our children, let's have certain criteria for what and how many we purchase. Finally, giving children responsibility for a certain amount of money teaches them how much those coveted toys cost. The children begin to learn the value of money and can start to set good patterns for buying and saving that will last a lifetime.

Does Your Child Really Need It?
DONALD & NAOMI COLE

WE HAD THE ADVANTAGE OF BRINGING UP OUR CHILDREN in Africa where many of the people lived a subsistence existence. It was a marginal life and the possession of a shirt or two was evidence of prosperity.

When we came back to the States, what our kids needed and wanted was very different from what they needed and wanted in Africa. We need to remember that children are, in fact, a part of their culture, and needs vary from one culture to another.

This problem is not limited to children. How many adult American Christians have come to grips with the question of distinguishing between needs and wants and have actually solved the problem?

In Don's work in Africa, his clothing needs were extremely simple. But when we returned to the United States and Don began a ministry with Moody Bible Institute that required a certain amount of contact with the public, his clothing needs changed. He had to wrestle with, "What kind of suit do I need? Where do I buy it? What kind of home do I need?"

The answers vary from culture to culture. Because Don works in downtown Chicago, he lives more or less like an average businessman or college professor. He is indistinguishable from his peer group. Is this right or wrong? We don't think it is necessarily wrong, but we don't think all of these questions are going to be answered until we get to heaven.

One essential quality to teach is stewardship. Don recalls,

"When I was thirteen, I got a job as a newsboy. I'll never forget my father's reaction when I showed him the pile of quarters and dimes I earned my first week. He looked it over and said, 'Good, how much are you going to give to God?' I hadn't thought of giving God anything. But I started."

Christmas or birthdays are times when you can meet some "wants." It's a perfect opportunity to find out and give what will really please your children. We remember one Christmas we decided not to give our kids any gifts, but to give money we would have spent on presents to those in real need. While it was certainly a noble idea, when Christmas came we felt terrible that we had neglected the children, and we found something to give them.

We enjoy giving gifts. Naomi likes going out and looking for something that our daughter wants, but doesn't really need. "I enjoy trying to find something she would really like. It is a token of my love for her."

Helping Kids Use Money Wisely
BRUCE BARTON

AS IN SO MANY OF THE PRINCIPLES FOR GUIDING TEEN-agers, financial planning concepts should be taught to children at all ages. However, many basic principles about money that you have taught your children can be refined and upgraded in the teenage years.

Guiding your children about money offers you as parents the opportunity to teach them an increased sense of responsibility and self-reliance. It provides tremendous opportunity for teenagers to learn how to make good choices. Teenagers can put money in its proper perspective as a resource for life-management and not as an end in itself. First Timothy 3:3 teaches that we should be free from the "love of money."

1. *What is money management?* Money management is "planning and using money to obtain what you need and want." There's nothing uniquely Christian about having and using money; however, Christians bring an additional attitude to their finances—stewardship. We are instructed in Scripture to be re-

sponsible stewards of the gifts given to us. Trouble starts when "stewards" begin to act like "owners." A good steward manages his resources well, knowing ultimately they belong to Someone else and must be used for a greater purpose. On the other hand, an owner has complete control. He may choose to hoard or to waste his resources. As Christians, we do not have the sole ownership of our resources.

2. *Developing a spending record.* Young people can develop a tracking system to record where money comes and goes. The best way to begin a time-management plan is to write down how time is spent every half hour throughout the day for a three-week period. The same thing is true in developing a spending record. Write down how money is spent for an entire month, noting every expense and every income item. At the end of the month, review it to see what can be learned from that record. You can set up the three-column monthly journal to record income, expenses, and balance.

As you can see from the example, a sheet can be developed on notebook paper or you can purchase a three-column monthly journal from a stationery store. The month and the opening balance, all the money the young person has in his possession at home, is listed at the top. A description of the item, whether income or expense, is listed with the date. For each entry on the page, an amount is written either in the income or expense column, and a running balance is listed in the far-right column. At the end of the month, the closing balance is written at the bottom of the page. This will be the opening balance for the next month. After a one-month period has passed, the young person should review his *expenses* and categorize according to the following:

- Tithing
- Savings—future education, trips
- School—activities, lunches, carfare, books
- Personal—grooming, cosmetics, jewelry, clothing, sports equipment, repairs of sports equipment
- Gifts
- Entertainment—dates, movies, sports events, records, food

When the expenses are categorized, the teenager will have a very clear idea where the money is currently being spent.

3. *Set up a system for budgeting.* Once you determine where

MONTHLY JOURNAL

| Month _____ |
| Opening Balance $47.50 |

Date	Description	Income	Expense	Balance
1/13	Allowance	3.00		50.50
1/15	Baby-sitting	5.00		55.50
1/16	Pizza after game		3.00	52.50
1/17	Folders for class		2.00	50.50
1/20	Allowance	3.00		53.50
1/21	Deposit to savings account		45.00	8.50
	Closing Balance $8.50			

the money is going, then you can determine a plan for where it ought to go. This can be done by allocating percentages of income to the established categories. For example, once the monthly income is established, the young person could say, "I am going to allocate ten percent of my income for tithing, fifteen percent of my money will go for savings, twenty-five percent for entertainment, twenty-five percent for personal, twenty percent for school, five percent for gifts." That kind of a very basic budget can be set, then can be reviewed for several months to see whether or not these percentages are realistic.

4. *Establish goals for saving.* One of the main reasons young people don't save is that they fail to establish goals for their savings plan. If a person does not have a goal for his savings program, all he is doing is accumulating money. Young people will save more if the money is to be used for future education,

HOW IMPORTANT IS MONEY?

It is interesting to me that Jesus had more to say in the Bible about money than any other subject, which emphasizes the importance of this topic for my family and yours. He made it clear that there is a direct relationship between great riches and spiritual poverty, as we are witnessing in America today. Accordingly, it is my belief that excessive materialism in parents has the power to inflict enormous spiritual damage on their sons and daughters. If they see that we care more about things than people . . . if they perceive that we have sought to buy their love as a guilt-reducer . . . if they recognize the hollowness of our Christian testimony when it is accompanied by stinginess with God . . . the result is often cynicism and disbelief. And more important, when they observe Dad working fifteen hours a day to capture ever more of this world's goods, they know where his treasure is. Seeing is believing.

James Dobson

From *Dr. Dobson Answers Your Questions*, by James Dobson, Tyndale House Publishers, Inc. © 1982. Used by permission.

for a special trip, or for some special sports equipment. Have your teen establish a savings account, and make a practice of depositing his money in the bank whenever enough has been accumulated that it is no longer wise to keep it at home. Many teenagers establish monthly savings deposit plans. If your teen is employed, he should be encouraged to deposit some portion of his check into a savings account each time he is paid.

5. *Teach the principle, "Never overspend."* A main principle of financial planning is never to spend more than you make. Sounds simple, but think how many people spend more than their incomes. By keeping track of where money goes and by establishing a basic budget system, the young person can learn not to overspend. Parents may have to pitch in and help when there is

an unusual expense, a repair, or some unanticipated item that neither his allowance nor his income can handle. For example, if your teen is playing football and accidentally breaks a window, the cost of repairing it might be greater than he can stand. You may want to help out. Parents need to be realistic and flexible to help teens through rough times.

6. *Reward your teenager for staying on a budget.* You may want to begin by reviewing his budget with him on a monthly basis. If the teenager stays on budget for that month, then give him permission to spend some portion of the money he has accumulated. Your options are to reward him with praise or with some extra income. Allow him to live with the natural consequences of his spending—when he runs out of money he has nothing more to spend.

7. *Correct impulsive buying.* If your teenager is an impulse buyer, here are some suggestions you might make.

● Before the teenager can purchase an item that he wants, he must get three separate prices from three separate stores.

● Make an impulsive buying list. To use an impulsive buying list, all the items desired for purchase must be written down. Then have the teenager list them in order of priority. In order for an item to be purchased, it must stay in the number one spot for thirty days. If, for example, she wants to buy a pair of jeans, the jeans must be number one on the list for thirty days. If halfway through the thirty-day period, she decides she'd like a new hairdryer; then that hairdryer must stay number one on the impulse list for thirty days before it can be purchased. This will help spread out impulsive purchases. This would primarily apply to items that are not normally budgeted and are not routine purchases.

As you work with your teenager on his financial plan, a good approach to take is to suggest and guide rather than to direct and boss. If you can function as his financial adviser, he can learn good principles. The results will be rewarding.

C H A P T E R
5

How Do I Help
My Child Deal with
Substance Abuse?

Preparing Your Child
for a Drinking Society
DAVID VEERMAN

CHRIS IS FROM A STRICT BAPTIST FAMILY WHERE ALCOHOL
is banned. In high school, though, his continued success on the
football field provides a reason for postgame celebrations with
his teammates. A drinking habit is the result.

"I feel so rotten." he confides, "I don't want to drink. My
parents would kill me if they ever found out."

According to a recent survey, 24 million high school students
drink, 75 percent of them regularly, and 1 out of every 5 seniors
admits being drunk at least once a week. Alcohol leads marijuana
as the most abused drug on campus.

The results are devastating. *Better Homes and Gardens* magazine reports that more than 4,000 teenagers will be killed this
year, and more than 40,000 teenagers will be injured because
they mix driving with drinking. Teenage drinking affects most
American homes, including many Christian ones.

Children learn that drinking is an accepted American social institution by observing either their parents or people on television. Situation comedies laugh at drinking, advertisements plug it, dramas make it a mysterious god, talk-show hosts laugh with guests about their drinking bouts. Even the strictest, nonalcoholic family cannot shield its children from this reality. A child's curiosity is built by the mystery and excitement of "grown-up" beverages.

What can Christian parents do? Our actions fall into two areas: prevention and response.

To prepare your child for a drinking society, first ask yourself, "What does my life preach?" Regardless of what you say, your example will teach most.

The older I become, the more I realize how much I am like my dad. When I discipline my children, familiar phrases roll off my tongue, words I heard many times but never thought I would repeat. My father modeled life for me and was the only father I witnessed in action. Now the cycle continues, and I know my children will mirror me. This is a tremendous responsibility.

If you drink to relax or to make life more bearable, don't be surprised if your child turns to alcohol too. We are hypocritical if we expect our sons and daughters to be straighter or more spiritual than we are.

Marty's mother and brothers watched helplessly as his alcoholic father withdrew from them, stole from the family business, and destroyed himself, bottle by bottle. After a Campus Life meeting one evening, Marty poured out his frustrations and bitterness. Marty's turning point came when he realized he was becoming like his father by drinking to escape problems and stress. Marty gave his life to Christ, and God's life-changing process began.

Second, communicate with your child. The media presents alcohol as fun. Your task as parents is to balance the picture. Explain at a level he can understand what alcohol does and what motivates drinking. Answer questions honestly, even the embarrassing ones about Uncle Bob or Daddy's business friends.

Search the Bible together to see what God's Word teaches about alcohol. Teenagers especially need to know how the Bible says we should treat our bodies (1 Cor. 6:19-20), who should control our lives (Eph. 5:18-20), the example we should be for others (1 Cor. 10:23–11:1), and our responsibility to be good stewards of God's gifts (Matt. 25:14-30).

Third, take the time to develop a close relationship with your child from an early age. As he matures, he will be open to your counsel and more likely to come to you when he faces problems and temptations.

Prevention is great, you may say, but what do we do when the problem hits home? How should we respond when we find that our child has a drinking problem?

Even when confronted with the evidence, many parents deny that their teen could be involved with alcohol or drugs. And one form of denial is blaming others, often the son's or daughter's friends. "It isn't Scott's fault," they tell each other. While a teen's peers may reinforce bad behavior, they really reflect his or her problems; they don't cause them. And if parents continue to be blind to their son's or daughter's drinking problem, this hinders help.

At the other extreme, parents may blow up when faced with the evidence. This only serves to alienate and polarize. It may be a natural response, but it aggravates the situation.

Balance is the answer. Without falsely accusing, face the facts. Don't close your eyes to the problem. Don't come on too strong.

If this is your teen's first offense, talk it over with him and try to discuss *why*. Describe your feelings without attacking. Even if it is a repeat occurrence, be "slow to speak and slow to anger" (James 1:19). This does not mean that firm discipline is out, but your goal should be to keep communication channels open and find answers together.

Be honest with yourself too. Are you genuinely concerned for your teen or are you more worried about what your own peers will think and say? Or perhaps you feel guilty, believing you've failed as parents. Your teen has to believe you accept him and want the best for him, regardless of the cost to you, before he will be open to your counsel and guidance.

Drinking is not the real problem. Usually it is a symptom of poor self-esteem or a need for peer acceptance. Use this crisis as a chance to reaffirm your acceptance. Embrace him and let him know his worth and your love. This can be a dramatic life-changing turn toward deeper communication.

John was caught by school officials drinking in the parking lot with friends at a football game. He was terrified. What would his parents do?

They didn't hide their hurt or anger. But they also showed their love and concern. Hours of talking, confessing, weeping, and praying deepened their relationship. John still faced discipline, but he learned a valuable lesson—his parents really cared and wanted to understand.

It's common for parents to want to bear this burden privately for fear of what others may think. The Bible says to "bear one another's burdens" (Gal. 6:2). Selectively share your needs with your pastor and with Christian friends. They will offer prayer, counsel, and information. It is likely they have experienced similar situations, and certainly your pastor has counseled other parents. The church is strongest when it loves (John 13:35). Give it a chance.

Why Do Teenagers Smoke?
TIMOTHY SKRIVAN

OVER THE PAST FOUR OR FIVE DECADES NEW ISSUES HAVE faced parents, including drugs, the availability of birth control, and rock and roll music. One issue hasn't changed. That is concern about young people smoking cigarettes.

Information on the harmful effects of smoking has been accumulating over the years. Even with the conclusive evidence that smoking is a serious danger to health, one-fifth of all high school graduates are addicted to cigarettes, specifically to nicotine. (All statistics are courtesy of the American Cancer Society.)

Similar to the clothes one wears or the hairstyle one chooses, smoking is a statement of *who I am*. Let's take a look at what a teen is trying to communicate through the use of tobacco:

● *I belong.* Almost universally, the first time a young person smokes is in a group situation. Nicotine is a poison and usually causes nausea the first few times of smoking. It takes encouragement from friends and some perseverance to get to the point of enjoying or craving cigarettes.

- *I am grown up.* There are very few adults who would judge a young person's maturity by the amount of tobacco consumed because adults see maturity in relationship to responsibilities. Children, on the other hand, view maturity in terms of privileges. We communicate that smoking is an adult privilege.
- *I am tough.* No one wants to feel that people are taking advantage of him. One of the ways a person protects himself is by letting others know he is tough. Smoking communicates toughness to other people; even the brands of cigarettes communicate various degrees of toughness.
- *I am angry.* Many young people are growing up angry. The reasons are many, and the focus of the anger may be toward authority, parents, or themselves. When a teen is angry, smoking may be used to hurt someone.

The final reason young people smoke is that it is truly an *addiction.* Once smoking has left the experimental stage and has become a habit, there is a very definite addiction to nicotine. Heart rate, digestion, blood pressure, sleep, and temperature are all affected by smoking. The body becomes "used" to functioning with the drug and does not want to revert to functioning without it.

Eighty-five percent of all smokers wish they could quit. The evidence that smoking is harmful is overwhelming. It is reinforced when a teen's lifestyle is affected by bouts of coughing and short-windedness at an age when he should be at the peak of health.

The solution at face value is simple: the risks of smoking need to outweigh the benefits. However, the desire to quit smoking has two enemies—the addiction and the statement that is being made. Addiction may be easier to solve than "the statement." Ninety-five percent of people who quit smoking do it "cold turkey." They do not need the aid of pills, shocks, or counseling. They are willing to make the statement of who they are in less destructive ways and combat their addiction to nicotine.

As adults and parents, we do not want to see our children grow up "chained" to a destructive habit. In combating this difficult problem, our goal should be to teach our teens the ability to enjoy and express their uniqueness constructively.

Playing with Drugs Is No Game
GREGORY MONACO

OVER SEVEN MILLION PEOPLE IN THIS COUNTRY HAVE tried PCP, an animal tranquilizer that disorients, causes hallucinations, and sometimes kills. PCP is the third most widely abused drug, behind alcohol and marijuana.

A recent New York study of two million students revealed that 276,000 of them had tried PCP and 12,000 were using it ten or more times a month. Today alcohol seems to be replacing pot as the choice of drug users, but by no means have drugs disappeared. With a rising tide of evidence relating to heart, lung, brain, and reproductive system damage, drugs are still an overwhelming force to be reckoned with. In a recent national survey, one out of every ten high school seniors said he was using marijuana about once a day.

And if that isn't evidence enough, the "head shop" business—the sale of drug related paraphernalia—has annual sales of almost 1.5 billion dollars. Add to this the multi-billion dollar alcohol industry and you can see what our young people are up against.

So what does all this mean to you as parents? Let's look back at some statistics. One out of every ten high school seniors uses pot on a daily basis; three out of every four junior and senior high students are drinkers, one out of every five a problem drinker; one out of every eight students in New York has tried PCP.

The odds are good then that your son or daughter will at least try drugs or be in close contact with someone who does. A student in one city said dealing drugs was so easy it was funny. He sold all over school—in the bathroom, the hall, even through a window of a class in progress.

Here in my quiet suburb of Chicago, a respectable place, two drug busts took place this winter. One involved two million dollars worth of cocaine. The other involved a "mom and pop" business selling bags of marijuana out of their townhouse. The bags which were marked with Disney stickers were being sold to elementary school students! The worn-out excuse that "everyone does it" is becoming dangerously close to reality.

As parents, what can you do if you suspect your teenager is using drugs? Here are some suggestions:

1. First, don't deny your suspicions. Addiction to any drug takes time, but the younger abuser has a faster rate of addiction than the adult. What may take years for an adult can take only months for a teen; therefore, if you suspect your teen is using drugs, act on your suspicions. Don't hope it will go away, and don't deny the obvious. You are only giving up precious time.

2. Learn to recognize danger signals—the symptoms of drug abuse. Your local hospital, youth agency, or high school counselor can supply you with this information.

3. Deception and secrecy are two of your major foes. Remove the cloak of secrecy from your child's actions by talking with his friends' parents, his teachers, and even your neighbors. This assumes, of course, that you are willing to put his welfare above your personal embarrassment. Remember, you didn't cause the problem, but you can prevent the cure out of pride.

4. Be consistent. Develop clear rules in the areas of curfew, accountability for allowance, and where your teen spends his time. Then stick with them. Sometimes it's best to do this with the help of your pastor, some friends, or another supportive third party. This keeps you from overreacting and allows you to lend support when it comes time to follow through.

5. Become involved in community efforts to combat drug abuse. Contact your school or your city or county government to find out if your community has a task force on drug abuse. If it does, join it. If it doesn't, get one started.

6. Most importantly, keep lines of communication open with your child. Know what you are talking about. Discuss your plan with other helpers to ensure your objectivity before you talk to your child.

7. Finally, be ready for a tough time, and don't get discouraged or quit if you don't seem to be making headway at first. Your unconditional love is a force even more powerful than drugs.

CHAPTER
6

How Do I Help
My Child See Christ
in My Home?

Parents Set the Spiritual Pace
V. GILBERT BEERS

THERE IS SOMETHING IN PARENTING THAT IS MORE THAN principles. You may buy every book about parenting, catalog every principle, memorize the list, and even do your best to put these principles into your teen's life. But there is something lost in translation unless principles become flesh and blood, heart and mind, and live themselves out in your life. To put it bluntly, parenting cannot be reduced to a list of principles.

From childhood, we learn best from role models. Principles mean little to a child. Example means everything. "Do as I say, not as I do" is more than a joke. It is an oft-repeated tragedy in homes where parents believe their admonitions will be sufficient for their children. But children are perceptive, often more perceptive than adults, so words are easily canceled by conduct. We say, "God listens with concern to every prayer." But if we as parents are too busy to listen to our children, how then can they understand a God who hears?

63

"God is a loving Father," we say. But if we fathers are less than loving to our children, how then can our children relate to their Father in heaven as a loving Person?

"The Bible is the most important book in the world," we say. But if our children never see or hear us read it, how then can they relate what we say and what we do?

"The fruit of the Spirit is . . . " and we name them all. But if our children look in vain for love, joy, peace, and the other fruit in our lives, how then shall they understand our words?

"Christ changes our lives," we say. But if our children watch us "cut corners" and compromise integrity in little ways, how shall they know that we will not do the same in things that matter most, those that relate to our faith?

Words are extensions of life, not vice versa. We do not seek to fulfill what we have spoken, but rather speak what we have become because we believe it so completely. If we do not fully believe in or practice what we say, our children will quickly detect it.

Never think that children won't observe inconsistencies among belief, words, and conduct. They will probably know something is wrong before we do.

As parents, we seek to live consistent Christian lives, not merely to set a good example for our children, but because we believe this pleases our Lord. Not only that, it must surely please a Christian wife or husband. Consistent Christian living will make you and me happier, more balanced persons, for our belief and words and conduct will be in harmony.

When all of that is happening, we will catch the attention of our children and focus it on the living Christ. An ounce of loving role modeling is worth a pound of parental pressure.

What Kind of Spiritual Example Are You Setting?
ADRIAN ROGERS

A JUVENILE DELINQUENT IS USUALLY NOTHING BUT A CHILD who's trying to act like his parents. Society's dropouts are not primarily the children, but the parents who have failed to be the kind of example they should have been.

Adam and Eve, the first parents, were not the best examples to Cain and Abel. Eve, for example, had a wrong set of values. I see many mothers today with the same values Eve had in the Garden of Eden. First, she valued physical gratification. She "saw that the tree was good for food." Second, she valued aesthetic stimulation. She saw that "it was pleasant to the eyes." Third, she valued intellectual investigation. It was "a tree to be desired to make one wise" (Gen. 3:6, KJV).

I think the same values are prominent today. There's nothing wrong with physical gratification, with caring for the body; but we are living in a day when parents are pampering the body while strangling the soul. Aesthetic stimulation is not bad in itself, but I know parents who would give up going to church before they would give up their new color television. When they do go to church, their primary interests are in the flower arrangements, the art, the lawn, the fashion, the furniture, and so on.

Likewise, intellectual investigation is good unless it becomes the motivating factor. So many people today are worldly wise but spiritually ignorant. Eve sold her soul to satisfy her curiosity, and her values filtered down to Cain and Abel.

Not only did those boys have a mother with the wrong set of values, they also had a father with no backbone. Adam was intended to be the head of the house, but he left his rightful place. Eve was to be his helpmate, but Adam let her lead him.

I've been a pastor for many years, and I have yet to see a home where the wife and children did not follow the man if he, from the beginning of the marriage, loved and served God. As a general rule, if the home is wrong, it's because the man is wrong, because he has abdicated his place of leadership. I am convinced that if a home is wrong, God holds the man responsible.

So Eve's values were wrong, Adam had no backbone, and Cain and Abel were just left to chance. One boy went right, and one boy went wrong. Inconsistent living brings inconsistent results.

How should parents set good examples? One of our major duties is to start early. I have observed that many parents start sixteen years and 175 pounds too late. According to Proverbs 19:18 that we're to chasten our son while there's hope. Sometimes we're going to find ourselves in a hopeless situation if we don't start early enough. Proverbs 22:6 (KJV), "Train up a child in the way he should go: and when he is old, he will not depart from it," implies that we're to give him the training when he's young. The earlier we start, the better.

Then, if we are going to be good examples, we have to have strong values. Because of the world's humanistic philosophy, teenagers need definite values. They need a code to live by; they need to learn what is right and what is wrong in concrete terms. This is right and that is wrong because God says so. You see Mom and Dad living this way because the Bible teaches that this is the way we're to live.

Even games are no fun without boundaries. So many young people today don't know where the boundaries are. They have no distinct guidelines. These young people need a code to live by, a creed to believe in, something that's not just sentimentality but that is explainable and spiritually authenticated in their hearts and lives. They need to say, "The Bible is the Word of God; Christ is the Son of God; and there is indeed victory in Christ."

Not only do they need a code to live by and a creed to believe in, they also need a cause to serve. So many young people are "at sea" today because they don't have a cause. Young people today are looking for involvement. If we as parents have a soft religion, we're not going to offer any challenge.

We parents need to start early; we need to build strong values; and we need to show love. Teenagers, more than anybody else on the face of the earth, need love. I think they're more interested in love than anything else, and parents need to show love by touching them appropriately and often. Not only do parents need to show love to their teenagers, they also need to demonstrate it to each other. We've all heard the saying that the best thing a father can do for his teenager is to love that teenager's mother.

We also need to use discipline. According to Proverbs 13:24 that if we spare the rod, we hate our son. So often the parents will say, "I don't discipline him because I love him so much." But in truth, we don't love him if we don't discipline him; we love ourselves and don't want the problem of discipline. We don't want to risk the child's displeasure.

Fathers need to be careful that they don't try to be just another brother. Teenagers don't need more buddies; they have plenty already. They don't need leaders; they develop their own.

BE WHAT YOU BELIEVE

Not all children raised in Christian homes are on fire for the Lord. Some parents, wishing to avoid conflict, tend to back off from religious topics as their children get older. I think this is unwise. But some ways are more effective than others for reaching our older children for the Lord.

We have to model what we believe. If we want our children to be soul-winners, they need to see it in our lives. We can also expose them to other people who are good models, people who are not only living attractive, radiant lives, but who are also witnessing for Christ. We can do more through teaching than through preaching, more through example than through demands.

It is also helpful to take them to a good church for worship and praise meetings where there is excitement and enthusiasm for the Lord expressed in good taste. Look for a place where God is truly loved and worshiped and adored, where there is a lot of singing and where there are a lot of testimonies of how Christ is answering prayer and changing lives. I am a strong believer in testimonies, especially if they are given by people our children respect.

We need to expose our children to aggressive, vital, dynamic Christianity and continue to pray for them. Prayer accomplishes more than anything else.

Bill Bright

The one thing they really do need is parents who are examples, who will live the Gospel in front of them.

Yet not everything can be taught by example. We need to teach empirical truths and biblical facts. Jesus, the master

Teacher, practiced what He preached and preached what He practiced; that's what made Him such a great Teacher. One without the other is not enough.

Young people need consistency. To be consistent doesn't mean to be perfect. Rather, it means holding firm to your goals, your standards, your aspirations. Then, when you fail, you confess and go right back to trying to live by your standards. I've failed many times. I've lost my temper with my children; I've been rude to their mother. I've done things that are un-Christlike and unworthy of the Lord I serve. But by God's grace, I have been enabled to confess not only to the Lord, but also to my family. And the wonderful thing is that my confession does not lessen their respect for me. To the contrary, it increases their respect for me.

I don't have to pretend to be perfect; they already know I'm not. But if they see that my confession is honest, then they know that at least I'm real. I'm not a hypocrite. That's how I can be consistent without being perfect, and how I can keep my children's and my wife's respect.

Religious Homes vs. Christian Homes
RICHARD HALVERSON

I GREW UP IN NORTH DAKOTA WITH SOME PRECONceived ideas about the church and its influence in the home. Though my mother had met the Lord in a Billy Sunday evangelistic meeting and attended church regularly, she never told me that God loved me and Christ died for me. She did as much as a mother could to bring us up in church, but my father never attended. My grandfather had no respect for preachers either, so I grew up believing that preachers were failures and only women and children went to church. Later, in my teenage years, I got the feeling that to be religious I had to refrain from smoking, drinking, going to shows, dancing, and playing cards.

In evaluating my youth, I believe I was brought up in a religious home rather than a Christian home. This kind of legalistic environment is less than biblical. In fact, I would venture to say that the primary difference between a religious home and a Christian home lies in the extent of legalism versus genuine intimacy and communication of God's love.

Many teenagers have been turned off to Christianity as a result of religious training in the home. In my own home, I tried to express my faith without forcing the issue. My children have memories of opening the door to my study and finding me on my knees. Though I never knew it until much later, the impact of this sight left them thinking of me as a man of prayer.

I tried to make sure that my children grew up in an open environment, not a legalistic one. My wife and I never allowed our children to think they had to be different or live differently than their peers because their father was a pastor.

I believe there are two major tasks for the parents who want to make their home truly Christian. The first is to show affection and love toward every member of the family. In fact, when I do premarital counseling, I always ask the following questions: "Do you think your father and mother loved each other? How did they show that love?" In my forty years as a pastor, I've discovered that some adults have never seen their own parents express affection to each other; nor have they experienced affection from either or both parents.

The father needs to show love to the mother and children, especially to daughters. If daughters don't get affection from their fathers, they grow up not knowing how to handle intimacy. One of the explanations for young girls getting involved in sex at a very early age is that they long for intimacy. Sexual involvement becomes a substitute for intimacy with their father.

The second task for parents who want a truly Christian home is to create a time for family devotions in a nonlegalistic atmosphere. Insisting on participation can alienate a teenager, yet every family should try to meet the Lord sometime each day.

Christian Homes, Christian Children?
ROSS CAMPBELL, M.D.

ALMOST 80 PERCENT OF THE CHILDREN BROUGHT UP IN Christian homes do not become Christians.

Many of the children who do become Christians want to be under authority. They want to be told what to do because they want to please. If you tell them exactly what you want from them, they will respond. These children look responsible, but what they are doing is not true responsibility. They are just carrying out commands because they want to make others happy. They become Christians to please their Christian parents.

Most children, however, do not have this type of personality. Fully 75 percent are just the opposite. They don't want to be under authority. In fact, they are antiauthority. They want to think for themselves and make their own decisions. They have an "I'd rather do it myself" attitude. When children like these are raised by Christian parents who use the authority of the church or the Bible to make the children do things their way, these kids rebel.

It is easy for this 75 percent to become passive-aggressive—to comply outwardly (what choice do they have?) but to devote their inner energies to being disruptive and hostile. It is easy for them to reject Christianity because they are not especially concerned with pleasing their parents and they don't want to be under anybody's authority, including Christ's. And yet these resistant children are the very ones who, if they become Christians, will be outstanding leaders in God's kingdom.

What can we do to prepare the soil of our children's hearts for the seeds of the Holy Spirit?

1. *Love them with a deep love.* By your love, your children learn to understand God's love. If they feel loved, they will not have to be depressed and angry because the rest of the world is mixed up. They will be able to respond to God's love.

2. *Teach your children to handle anger maturely.* If they know how to admit anger and resolve it, it will not come out in passive-aggressive, antiauthority behavior.

3. *Avoid pressuring your children, especially about religion.* As our children enter preadolescence and then adolescence, they work hard at becoming independent. Parents make a mistake if they are harsh and authoritarian during those potentially rebellious years. The child will react, "As soon as I can, I am going to reject every bit of this."

Many young teenagers don't want to go to church and show no interest in spiritual things. When this happens, parents often panic and begin to put pressure on their children. They lecture them, or they drop little remarks—"How can you call yourself a Christian?" or "You think you're a Christian; why don't you act like a Christian?"

But pressure only increases children's resentment about spiritual things. If they do not resolve their hostility by the time they must establish their own spiritual identity, they may well reject Christianity altogether.

MODELING YOUR FAITH

As parents, we are never sure when we might be modeling the Christian faith in an important way in front of our children. Once Jeremy, our youngest, was with me when I took a man out for coffee to help him with some difficulties. Through that, my son saw some of the elementary steps of sharing the faith.

Later that week Jeremy came to me and said, "Dad, I witnessed for the first time in my life." He had seen the naturalness of sharing Christ, and now he was ready to do it himself. In fact, he invited his friend to church with him the next week.

I hadn't realized what an impact my actions were having on him. Discipling and witnessing are simply important parts of my life, and now Jeremy is learning that way of life too.

David Mains

One of my sons went through an antispiritual stage. There was nothing I could do for him directly without increasing his resentment; I had to trust him to other adults outside the family and let them influence him. That was not easy to do, but I knew it would have been harmful to lecture him or discipline him.

Fortunately, we had good helpers. David was a macho football player, and his youth director, an ex-football player, related to him well. In addition, the football coaches at the public high school were active, dynamic Christians. So during those two difficult years when I could not talk about spiritual things around David, I could guide him so he was exposed to these men.

When David was sixteen and a half, he came down the aisle at church one Sunday morning and accepted Christ. I was completely surprised. It was one of the most thrilling moments of my life. I am convinced that he would not have made that decision if we had not given him the freedom to take his spiritual quest outside the family.

You're a New Christian Family: What Do You Do Now?
KENNETH GANGEL

SETTING UP A CHRIST-CENTERED HOME DOESN'T HAVE TO be a traumatic experience for new believers. You begin by trusting God, asking Him to make up for all the lost years of communication and friendship your family could have had. Then commit your home to the Lord with an attitude of expectancy: "Lord, we're starting from scratch and need to learn how to put You first."

The home then becomes a little school where everybody is growing and sharing with each other. As family members learn new things from God, they reinforce value choices and priorities. Parents should communicate openly with their children and not be afraid to admit when they fail.

It's important to immediately establish family devotions or worship time. Even new believers with limited Bible knowledge should start by opening up to a passage and asking each other, "What does this mean? What should we be doing about it as a family?" The Holy Spirit will help teach the family as they explore God's Word together.

Children may be surprised to see authoritarian parents humbling themselves and making themselves vulnerable. At first, there may be a credibility gap—kids will stand back and say, "Prove your faith and leadership; show me you can pull it off."

Instead of getting defensive, parents should admit that they are depending on Christ to help them with their weaknesses. There's nothing wrong with admitting to your children that you need help being a godly father. Scripture teaches us to be vulnerable: "Not that we are competent to claim anything for ourselves, but our competence comes from God" (2 Cor. 3:5, NIV).

When children see this kind of honesty, they're not likely to spit on it and say, "Do your own thing, and I'll do mine." Kids are ultimately more hostile to the authoritarian parent than to the vulnerable parent. There are no formulas guaranteed to swing children around to the parents' side, but openness and communication often work wonders.

A new Christian family should also strive to include children in decision-making. Instead of saying, "We're going to the lake this weekend" and giving kids no choice, parents should let children have a voice and ask them what they want to do: "Would you like to go to the lake this weekend, or would you rather do something else?" Parents, of course, have the ultimate responsibility under God to make the final decision, but children should have a voice in the process.

One of the things our family did was to plan family vacations together. We plotted out map routes and scouted out parks to visit. A parental duty—vacation planning—turned out to be family fun.

We also had a family council, a time when family members could discuss whatever they wanted. Sometimes the kids would say, "We'd like to call a family council because we feel we're being asked to go to bed too early." Then we would get together and negotiate the issue.

One issue that families should discuss is what church they would like to attend. After visiting several churches, they can talk about what they're looking for in a church and where they think God wants them. Parents and children may need to weigh the importance of their needs—they may end up choosing XYZ church because of its growing youth program, even though it has mediocre preaching.

But even though a church may not be perfectly suited to all your family's needs, family unity in worship is important. My daughter attends a college far away from the church I pastor, but we're working hard to make sure we're still all together on Sunday morning.

Ultimately, after family worship, devotions, and decision-making have been discussed, the family of new believers can have an easier time adjusting than parents who have been believers all along but have not applied their faith at home. Instead of living down sixteen years of hypocrisy, you're starting anew. And that's an exciting, not scary, experience.

The Powerful Effect of a Parent's Prayer Life
EVELYN CHRISTENSON

IN 1968, I WAS INVOLVED WITH A PROJECT ORGANIZING A telephone prayer chain. As the telephone would ring, my children watched me write down the request at the blackboard, hang up, and call the next person to start the chain. Then, I would go to prayer immediately. Thus, they were able to see the priority of prayer in my life and the discipline of stopping to pray no matter what was going on.

They also heard the phone ring and listened as the answers came in. This was a subtle example, and I didn't realize that they were paying much attention until they were older. But I knew what a tremendous impact this made on their lives when they began to ask for prayer if something was happening in their lives or in the life of a friend. They had watched the power of prayer in my ministry and my personal life, and it became a way of life for them.

Another part of my prayer life that affects my children is my intercession for them. I consider praying for my children to be the most significant thing I do for them. I spend, as a rule of thumb, two hours a day in prayer and they are at the top of my list. My motivation is that I believe God answers prayer. If I didn't, I wouldn't spend all that time praying.

When my daughter, Jan, took her internal medicine board tests, which involved eight hours of writing, two days in a row, I spent every hour in prayer for her. Only God knows what my life of intercession has done for my children, but prayer is a tremendous way we can help them, whether they are aware of it or not.

HOW TO PRAY FOR YOUR CHILDREN

What should parents pray for their teens? Most importantly, that God's will be done. This means that He will have His perfect will in them all day long, that He will be training them, making them holy, as He desires.

Sometimes this means praying for something hard to help a teen see his error, like "Lord, do whatever You need to do to turn that teen around." I've prayed that many times, but it is a difficult prayer because I know God might answer it by a hard experience.

My own mother prayed for my brother for twenty-seven years, and she finally said, "God, do anything You need to bring my boy back to You." A little while later, my brother was in a serious car accident. He survived it and through it came back to God, but that is still a scary prayer to pray.

Then, there are specific things parents can pray for. Perhaps the teen has a test that day in school. I don't pray for all A's, but "God, You know if this child's self-image is not what it should be and if he needs some encouragement. So give him the test results he needs." Or I pray, that if it is His will, that God would give my teen enough success to give him courage to enter into a certain field of study.

I also ask God to deliver my children from the evil one. I claim the blood of Jesus over them and tell Satan he doesn't have a right in my children's lives. If they are sinning, I ask God to rebuke them and pour coals of fire on their heads until they can't stand what they are doing. I probably pray some pretty peculiar prayers as a parent.

Evelyn Christenson

I reversed this process too, asking my children to pray for me. I admitted my needs to my children, even when they were young. I let them know that I didn't have it all together. I would tell them, "I'm scared; I have to do a program on TV, and I don't know how to do it. Would you pray for me?"

As we admit our needs to our children, it becomes much easier for them to admit their needs to us. In doing so, we're not queens or kings sitting high on thrones, but people who need to change and who need other people to pray for us.

Praying *with* our children is also extremely important. When they are small, praying together is easily structured—at mealtimes, at bedtime. Our family had the practice of praying with the kids just before they walked out the door to school, even if we only had time for one sentence. That prayer not only helped them, it set my mind at rest, knowing that I had handed over my children to God for the day.

As children become teens, they can shy away from prayer, thinking it's kid stuff. The secret is to pray little short sentence prayers, with the parents not praying any more than the teen. Then, the teen is made to feel that his prayers are just as important as his parents'. The teen has equal time and equal worth in prayer; this is helpful, though sometimes hard for parents to remember.

Parents could spend the rest of their lives reading good books on prayer. But the important thing is to pray, rather than learn more about prayer. God answers prayer, not the study of prayer.

Prayer takes discipline too. Sometimes it means giving up a TV program or some other leisure activity that is not bad in itself, but is not a top priority. We need to be willing to give up some of the little things we like to spend more time in prayer. I've had to make sacrifices in order to pray but it has been worth it.

A prayer partner can also help. If both parents are Christians, then this is a natural. If not, a parent can pray and ask God to show him someone with whom he can pray on a regular basis.

Dusting Off the Family Altar
DAVID VEERMAN

IMAGINE THIS. IT IS SUNDAY MORNING AND YOUR PASTOR has just asked for a show of hands of those parents who have a regular "family altar." How do you feel? A common response would be embarrassment and frustration, but mostly guilt.

Christian parents want to have a regular time of devotions, but most attempts end in failure or are met with a yawn. This is especially the case where teenagers are involved. Generally "underwhelmed" by the idea, they reluctantly participate, and that's only when they are home. School, church, and friends keep the social calendar full. Unfortunately, in many homes, the most consistent family togetherness occurs in front of the TV set. And, to be honest, there are times that parents just do not feel like mustering the energy it takes to prepare and motivate the family.

But family devotions are important. These experiences can be unifying, building the home on Christ. Children who grow in an atmosphere where Bible study and prayer play vital roles will see Christ as an integral part of their lives, and they will be inclined to build their homes on Him as well.

Teaching can also occur as parents take the lead in discovering scriptural truths instead of relying exclusively on Sunday School lessons and the pastor's sermons. As conscientious parents, we have a responsibility to plant our children in the faith (Prov. 22:6) and to nurture them (Matt. 19:13-15). It would be irresponsible to expect others to care for our children's total spiritual growth.

The home is the crucible of the Christian life. Sibling conflicts, growing pains, and other normal family tensions provide real tests of faith. In fact, the Apostle John implies that the home is the ultimate test. If a person hates his brother whom he has seen, how can he possibly love God whom he has not seen? (1 John 4:19-21) Families are falling apart all around us—we need the glue of God's presence to keep ours together. It may be difficult to have a family altar, but it is worth the effort.

Though most of us are convinced of the validity of the family altar, it is the "how to" which causes problems. However, it *can* be done! First, we must realize that "just trying" speaks volumes about us. Regardless of our success, the fact that we *want* to have family devotions illustrates our priorities. I can remember numerous attempts by my parents to have a consistent family altar. I don't recall which materials they used or much of the content they covered, but I know they tried. As Christian parents, they were convinced of the necessity of regular Bible study and prayer. They probably questioned many times whether their fidgety son heard very much, but I saw—and learned.

Second, we should be consistent. There is no formula for the frequency of family devotions. Many parents strive for a daily commitment, while for others, once a week is fine. Too often the

STEPS TO STARTING A FAMILY WORSHIP TIME

The spiritual training of children should begin in the home. If you and your children never worship together at home, you are missing one of the most rewarding experiences in life. Let me encourage you to develop a time of family worship every day. The following steps will get you started.

1. Begin when your children are young. If you haven't yet begun and your children are no longer young, begin now.

2. Select a specific time when you can meet consistently every day (first thing in the morning, at supper, right before bed, etc.).

3. Meet with your spouse ahead of time to plan and decide what to do during family worship time.

4. Have fun. Your children should worship because they *want* to—not because they *have* to.

5. Keep it short. The length of time will depend on the ages and spiritual maturity of the children involved, but fifteen minutes is usually plenty.

6. Use a good resource. "Walk Thru the Bible" has a daily devotional book called *Family Walk.* Other organizations also have quality products in this area.

7. Apply what you discuss to everyday life. After each meeting, ask, "What can you do today to practice what we just learned?" Then the next time you meet, follow up by asking, "How did your plan work out?"

8. Let your children share in leading the worship. High school teens should have regular leadership responsibilities, but even younger children can take part in smaller ways.

9. As your children get older, have them add a daily time with the Lord on their own. Then during family

worship, they can begin to share what God is doing in their lives on an individual basis.

These suggestions are only guidelines. You know your family better than anyone else does. Base your planning on what you think is best for them. Challenge each other to become not only the people God wants you to be in the world, but also to be the family He wants you to be at home.

Barry St. Clair

attempts are intense and sporadic. Dad will insist on devotions every day at dinnertime; but because of schedule conflicts and interruptions, this effort lasts about a week. Instead, we should decide in advance which days (and time of day) are best suited. Then we must follow through with few exceptions and insist that everyone is present. Consistency will produce expectancy and habit, and will reinforce the importance of the study.

Preparation is the third emphasis. If we believe in a family altar and want the teaching to be effective, "winging it" will not do. Also, it is a cop-out to say we are relying on the "Spirit's leading" as an excuse for our lack of preparation. Teenagers especially will see that we are only going through the motions. Adequate preparation includes choosing the appropriate topics and materials, thinking through the process, and praying for God's guidance. Paul instructs us to pray about everything (Phil. 4:6). We will not experience success depending on our strength alone. The content for our studies could include an inductive study of a book of the Bible, the scriptural teaching about a specific subject, biographies of biblical characters, or the writings of Christian authors, scholars, and theologians. Christian bookstores have a multitude of resources available: Sunday School quarterlies, collections of personal devotions, books by fascinating authors from C.S. Lewis to Joni Eareckson Tada, and more. Our ministers will give guidance here, perhaps even a preview of the sermon topics so that Friday's devotion will relate to Sunday's message. Whatever materials are chosen, they should be Bible-centered.

As we ponder the actual process of our devotions, let us remember *creativity*. The family altar is not a show to be programmed, but creative planning will heighten interest and facilitate learning. We can use illustrations, ask questions, tell a story (parable), or sing a song. Perhaps the whole family could draw a picture or assemble a puzzle. And what about the leader? Why not give our children opportunities to teach us? As they teach, we should be open to their lessons, accepting what is said and thanking them for their help.

Prayer should be a key ingredient in our devotions (not just punctuation at the beginning and end). We should allow time for each person to share requests. When we pray, we can vary the pattern—sometimes praying around the table, at other times using conversational prayer, and so on. Our vulnerability is vital for the prayertime. We should request and share real needs. (Compiling a list is helpful.) When God answers, the family can rejoice together. When my father took a job in another city, we prayed as a family about finding a house and a new church home. When God answered our prayers, I was excited and impressed. At five years old, I learned a valuable lesson.

The length of each devotional experience may vary, depending on the subject and leader. Bible study is the head, and prayer is the heart of the family altar. Both are necessary and should be included every time. This is important to remember when we plan.

Finally, we should emphasize personal application, each time discovering what changes we should make in our lives. These practical challenges are for everyone, parents included. We need to allow God to speak to us through His Word by continuing to look for His applications. This is not an opportunity to preach at our kids—we learn *together*. We should also remember that this is an individual and personal process, each family member seeking God's Word for his or her life.

The family altar will take time, commitment, creativity, and vulnerability. The results, however, can be invaluable—learning from God's Word, sharing ourselves with our children, building the home on Christ, and being eyewitnesses to God's work in the lives of those we love dearly.

C H A P T E R
7

How Do I Help
My Child Thrive
at School?

Choosing a School: Public,
Private, or Home?
PAUL HEIDEBRECHT

THE GROWTH OF CHRISTIAN SCHOOLS IS ONE OF THE
most significant developments in American education in recent
years. Increasingly, Christian parents are exploring alternatives to
the public schools. Some have become deeply involved in their
local Christian schools; others have begun to teach their children
at home. Many, however, still send their children to public
schools and attempt to exert a Christian influence in that arena.

The choice is not easy. Much depends on the type of schools
available to your family, as well as your own convictions about
the best way to prepare your children to live as Christians in our
society. Here are several different points of view.

● *The Christian school movement.* It's probably safe to call it
a movement because there is a new Christian school started
virtually every day. However, only 10 percent, or about 5 million, of the school-age children in this nation attend private

schools. Sixty percent of these are Roman Catholic. Over 1 million children are from conservative Protestant homes, and these attend a wide variety of schools from one-room, pastor-run schools in church basements to first-class residential academies.

There are two major streams in this Christian school movement. One is the Reformed tradition of Christian schools. This is well over 100 years old and has developed a rich philosophy of education. The other is the more conservative group that emerged in the 1960s and enjoys most of the publicity at the present time.

These two streams have much in common. Both are committed to a school curriculum that gives central place to the Bible. Both give high priority to the influence of Christian teachers, and both have the goal of fostering the growth of each student into mature Christian faith. But there are differences between these traditions as well.

The Reformed schools (and, to some degree, Lutheran schools) have always operated as an alternative system to the state-supported public schools. They have never been enamored with public education but have seen education as a matter of parental jurisdiction, not an activity to be controlled by the government.

Reformed educators have been interested in a holistic education that takes all aspects of human culture seriously and that invites students to think and act from a Christian perspective in contemporary society. They believe strongly in the importance of Christian community as well of living in relationship to the larger world as servants of Christ. Reformed educators are not interested in isolating their children from the world. To the contrary, they are obsessed with the task of equipping their children to be change agents in the world, equipped with the intellectual tools and a faith commitment to engage in the task of bringing all human culture under Christ's dominion.

Most conservative Protestant schools, on the other hand, have clearly arisen because of a relatively recent disenchantment with the public schools. Many date their "awakening" to 1963 when the Supreme Court ruled against prayer and Bible reading in the public schools. The conservative Christian community was shocked to discover that public schools were no longer promoting a mild form of Protestant faith and morality, but were actually espousing blatant secularism.

The schools that these Christians have erected since that time are in many ways like public schools of the past. They stress patriotism, basic skills, discipline, and the inculcation of moral values. These conservative schools are mainly interested in producing solid Christian citizens who can lead this nation through some process of spiritual renewal. Many do not possess the broad vision for Christian education that characterizes the Reformed schools. They are still primarily a protest movement and have yet to work out a positive rationale for what and how they teach.

Parents who send their children to conservative Protestant schools usually do so for two reasons. The most important one is that in a Christian school, children can be taught the Christian faith in all its dimensions. They can be given systematic instruction in the Bible. They are free to bring the biblical perspective into every subject. They can learn the habits of the Christian life such as prayer, service, and worship.

A second reason is the concern of many parents that in the public school, children will be exposed to influences that are either overtly evil or that are subtly detrimental. These influences can range from the availability of cigarettes, alcohol, and other drugs to the fact that God is not mentioned in any part of the school curriculum.

Christian school advocates also argue that their schools provide a better education. Many boast of their commitment to teaching the basics, of the higher test scores their students achieve, and of the higher percentage who enter college and eventually the professions.

Generally speaking, these claims are correct. Of course, it's not surprising. Families who support Christian schools are usually actively involved in helping their children learn. They show their concern for education by willingly making financial sacrifices for their children. Also, Christian schools tend to be blessed with smaller classes, allowing for more teacher-student interaction. And Christian schools are not overwhelmed by students with behavior disorders and learning disabilities. For these reasons, public school educators do not appreciate comparisons between public and Christian schools. Public school teachers are required to work under far more difficult conditions.

Finally, there is a political dimension to the Christian school movement. Many Christian school leaders see their schools as a breeding ground for a generation of Christians who will infect the secular culture with Christian thought and presence. This is how they apply the "salt of the earth" command Jesus gave us in the Sermon on the Mount. In their judgment, we cannot afford to turn our children over to a school system that promulgates a secular religion that rules out divine revelation and authority.

● *Home schooling.* Home schooling is the newest phenomenon on the educational scene. James Dobson calls it the wave of the future. No precise figures are available on its extent, but at least 500,000 children are being taught at home by their parents.

People who are interested in Christian schools are often the same people who investigate home schooling. Some Christian school organizations now provide an extension network for home schoolers.

Home schoolers share many of the concerns of the Christian school movement: disillusionment with public schools, concern for a genuinely Christian education, the desire to give their children a high-quality education. But they go further—they argue that children do better by staying at home longer. Too-early socialization of young children tends to make them dependent on their peers and less independent in their thinking. Long hours spent in classrooms are debilitating because of the boredom and routine. Many home schoolers have observed the conformist tendencies of school structures (public or Christian) and the subtle ways children are ranked, sorted, and channeled into particular tracks that control the direction of their lives. Too often individual creativity and initiative are stifled. Children learn to be docile, compliant citizens rather than rebels and leaders.

Home schoolers want to spend more time with their children, and they believe they can do a better job of teaching them than the schools can. In most cases, they are right. Given an adequate curriculum and an educated parent with personal concern for the children, it's rather hard not to succeed. In a few hours a day, a home-school educator can accomplish far more than a classroom teacher with thirty children.

Any parent who makes the commitment to teach children at home sets an example that we can only admire. We should congratulate such parents for bucking the system. Yet the same questions asked of Christian schools apply to home schools. Is it proper for Christians to withdraw from an arena where they can have an influence and be a help to other children? By keeping our children at home, do we reinforce a pattern of uninvolvement in the world which already characterizes too many Christians? Much will depend on the parents and how they live out their faith.

● *Christians in the public schools.* Let's look at the perspective of those Christians who keep their children in the public schools. In many cases, this is not a deliberate choice. The parents cannot afford the tuition for Christian schools. If funding were available to them, many would probably transfer their children to Christian schools. Yet there are many Bible-believing Christians who have made a conscious commitment to public education.

These parents tend to be fairly realistic about the public schools. They recognize the problems school districts face, but they point out the abundant opportunities for Christian parents to get involved in the life of the public school. They are disappointed when fellow Christians withdraw from the scene. For these parents, the public schools are a strategic point from which the Christian community can make an impact on the world.

Supporters of Christian schools argue that such Christian influence is vital, but that we can hardly expect our children to go into the public schools as witnesses to the Gospel. Supporters of public schools reply that the Christian witness is given by the entire family, not just the children. As parents interact with teachers, administrators, and other parents, their Christian values will become apparent.

Christians who send their children to public schools make several assumptions about public education. One is that the school has a limited educational task. It develops basic skills that everyone—Christian and non-Christian alike—must know in order to function in a modern democratic society. It is not expected to teach Christian faith or morals. The home and the church, not the schools, are the agencies of Christian education.

Another assumption that these parents make is that public education is essential in a democratic society. Private schools tend to perpetuate elitism and disunity, while public schools take children from all backgrounds and classes and offer them a learning experience in a genuinely democratic environment. These parents believe that children will learn to be tolerant of different beliefs and cultures by their exposure to them in public schools.

Finally, Christians within the public schools assume that normal Christian growth requires some direct involvement with the non-Christian world. Parents cannot prepare their children for Christian living by keeping them in an artificial environment where the distinctions between Christian and non-Christian are learned secondhand. Though always risky, it's far better to place children in a situation where they must make real choices, where being a Christian may involve some sacrifice, where service and outreach can be learned firsthand.

It would be interesting if someone were to study the results of Christian and public schooling on a segment of conservative Christian students to determine which approach produced stronger Christians. The results might be inconclusive because schooling is only part of the growth process. Such a study might lead to the same view that Andrew Greeley reached in his study of Catholic parochial schools: most children from strong religious families remained religious even when they attended public schools, but even parochial education could not preserve the religious interest of children from nonreligious or apathetic families.

School is tremendously important in the life of your child, but your home is even more important.

Who's Watching Your Kids?
JOHN WHITEHEAD

YOUR CHILDREN HAVE MANY AUTHORITY FIGURES OVER them, but the basic foundational authority belongs to you, the parents. All other authority is delegated. When a child goes to school, authority should be delegated to the teachers. Or after school, a coach might be responsible to act in place of the parents. The legal term (in Latin) for "in place of the parent" is *in loco parentis*.

Public schools used to be viewed as *in loco parentis*, but they have lost some of their authority lately. Some courts have upheld the requests of certain parents to prevent the teachers from having any real authority over their children. When parents refuse to delegate authority, they limit the ability of another person to regulate the activities of their kids.

But parents have a responsibility to delegate authority wisely. I even suggest that parents who have unmarried children in college encourage them to live at home while they go to school. College puts a lot of pressure on students—much of it anti-Christian. If they can come home to their parents and go to church with them, they will do much better in school. It was not uncommon in the Old Testament for children to live with their parents until they got married.

On a high school level, parents can take a personal interest in the people who share the authority over their teenager. In doing so, they may run into problems, but it is still well worth the effort to insure that their child gets the best training he can.

One common problem for Christian students is having to deal with a teacher who is not a Christian. If this is the case, the parents need to explain to the teacher that their child is a Christian, has certain biblical beliefs, and may possibly have to disagree with some of the material that is taught in the school. If the parents explain in a nice way, the teacher will usually try to respect the child's beliefs. I know of some recent instances where students refused to answer certain questions on a test about evolution because the "correct" answers went against their religious beliefs. I think teachers should respect the wishes of students not to answer in such circumstances.

Another occasional problem at school is the coach. Some coaches are so determined to win that they become overbearing and yell at the kids. If your child's coach gets out of hand, you need to have a talk with him. If he doesn't respond, you should take your teenager off the team. (And if your teen is a good athlete, the coach will sober up real fast.)

Again, the key is how you approach the coach. You need to explain that you are a Christian family, and you think there are better ways to motivate young people than yelling at them excessively. Try not to be defiant, or you will destroy your witness. Just tell him that your Christian principles teach you that people

QUESTIONABLE IDOLS

Our star-conscious society parades a smorgasbord of celebrities for our children to idolize. Of course, it's not wrong to look up to older "models"—we've all had our heroes. The problem is when these modern facsimiles espouse or encourage immoral and unchristian ideas and lifestyles. It makes us nervous to imagine our children becoming like them.

These are legitimate fears, but first we should analyze the situation and think through which values are being perpetuated. We should also look at the larger picture. The fact is that kids have idols because they are going through a time of role confusion and role sampling. In trying to find their identity, they emulate different people. Also, sometimes parents get too involved in underlying facts. For example, a rock star may have been married and divorced several times. Our kids may not even know that or care—they just like the music. We shouldn't assume that they believe in several remarriages.

The most helpful antidote is to spend time talking over this whole area with our kids. We should encourage them to evaluate the idol and to identify what they really want to emulate. (Is there a legitimate conflict of values?) In love, we can also help them see the logical conclusion of following a certain star and examine the subculture that he or she represents. When all is said and done, we need to be willing to accept a *modification* of the "hero-worship" and not a total rejection. Perhaps our greatest achievement will be to help them begin to think beyond "looks" and "sounds" to the deeper issues of values and lifestyles.

YFC Editors

are created in the image of God, and you just can't go along with using abuse—verbal or otherwise—to win games. I've coached teams so I find it easy to talk to coaches. But anyone can do it with a proper attitude.

Schools aren't the only places where parents need to be cautious about who has authority over their children. Sometimes, problems even arise at church where a pastor or youth minister is setting an example for your teen that goes against your family's values. What I have done in similar situations is to have the pastor over for dinner or tea and just talk to him. I also like to give him books that I think could help him in the area where we disagree.

Since the pastor is such an authority figure, it is important to approach him slowly and with respect if you feel he is doing something nonbiblical. Don't walk up to him and say, "Listen, I think you're a rotten sinner, and you need to repent right away." Wise parents will preface remarks before they confront the pastor with a point of disagreement.

Probably the most serious problems with authority over teenagers arise when one parent is a Christian and the other is not. It is one thing for two Christian parents to agree to take some action with a teacher, coach, or pastor who influences their child. But when one parent is in conflict with the other, the problem is not so easily settled.

I've had Christian wives come to me whose non-Christian husbands were abusing them—some physically and others only verbally (about their religion). No woman should allow her husband to beat her up, but verbal abuse is another matter. According to 1 Corinthians 7:14, an unbelieving husband can be sanctified through his wife. A Christian parent should go out of his (or her) way to be a positive influence to his spouse and to their teen.

I know a very good Christian lady who was having problems with her non-Christian husband. She had a job and he didn't, so she was expecting him to do some of the household chores while she was working. He thought it was her duty to clean the house, so they were fighting a lot. I advised her to stop confronting her husband and to just come home, hug him, and show him that she loved him. She tried it, and their relationship grew a lot stronger. The basic thing to remember if you are a Christian married to a non-Christian is to be the best spouse and parent you can possibly be. You may have to draw the line at how much you will give in to the other, but you should let your Christian light shine within your household whenever you can.

In all your relationships with other people who have authority over your child(ren), you must be open about your Christian feelings and beliefs. But above all, you must be compassionate. The burden is on you to be the most excellent parents you can be and so impress any other people who are over your teenagers so that they will listen to what you have to say.

The Rights of Christian Students in Public Schools
JOHN WHITEHEAD

A PUBLIC SCHOOL IN LUBBOCK, TEXAS WAS ONCE TAKEN to court because of a policy it had that allowed students to meet a half hour before classes started to discuss religious, ethical, or moral problems. The court ruled that such a policy was a violation of the First Amendment. The decision was upheld on appeal, and the Supreme Court refused to hear the case.

I'm currently involved in a case in Lake Worth, Florida where a public school principal reacted strongly to a page he saw in the yearbook. The picture was of a Bible club that had been on campus for twenty-five years. But the principal was so opposed to its presence at school that he kicked the club off campus and called in his staff of teachers to cut the pictures out of the yearbooks with razor blades. The principal's reaction was so spontaneous that he didn't even look to see what was on the other side of the page. As a result, the school had to reprint pictures of the Spanish Club as inserts.

Christians should be treated equally under the law, but that doesn't seem to be the case in many instances today. The apparent attitude in schools these days is that everybody is equal except religious people—especially Christians. We need to stress that we *do* have the same rights to have a club on campus as any other club in school. If it is within the law to have a Charles Darwin club, or whatever, it should also be legal to have Christian organizations on campus. And if it is OK to talk about popular sports figures over lunch, why should religious discussions be banned?

Yet some schools even prohibit teens from praying over their lunches. A lot depends on the attitude of the principal. Many are under pressure from non-Christian groups, such as American Civil Liberties Union. Christians must be aware of their rights. Let me review a few of them.

One right is what I call *accommodating neutrality,* and is based on the First Amendment. The idea is that the government should accommodate or assist religion whenever it can. If it doesn't *assist* religion, it becomes *hostile toward* religion. The latter would definitely seem the case for Christians who can no longer pray over lunch hour, talk about God on a public school campus, or have a Christian club. Therefore, we are not being treated fairly—accommodated—by the state. Such treatment is a violation of the First Amendment right to freedom of religion.

A 1969 Supreme Court decision ruled that high school students have the same rights as adults in public schools, with two conditions: (1) they cannot disrupt the orderly operation of the school, and (2) they cannot invade or violate the rights of others. As long as those two criteria are met, any Christian student has a right to say what he wants to say in the area of free speech.

The test case that led to the decision was a result of students wearing black armbands to protest the Vietnam War. They refused to take them off at the principal's request, so he suspended them. The case went to court and the students won. The Supreme Court ruled that the armbands were so closely related to free speech that the students must be allowed to wear them.

The same principle would apply, for instance, if a Christian student has a cross around his neck. He has a right to wear that cross as long as he doesn't violate the two conditions mentioned previously. He has a right to freedom of speech in public schools. He has a right to associate with his peers as anyone else would. The freedom of association guaranteed by the First Amendment applies to the Christian student every bit as much as to non-Christian students.

Students have the right to free speech, but they also have the right to hear. Let me explain. One hypothetical case people use is that citizens of the Soviet Union have a right to free speech, but only in the areas where nobody else can hear what they have to say. If students don't have the right to hear, they don't truly have free speech.

I have suggested that students start Christian clubs, Bible clubs, C.S. Lewis clubs, or the like, and then demand their constitutional right to hear the information that will be presented at these meetings. The Fourteenth Amendment says that everybody should be treated equally under the law, no matter if they are religious or not.

A myth has been perpetrated since the 1940s that anything religious on public property is automatically unconstitutional. A lot of courts and judges seem to have started believing this myth. But our founding fathers didn't believe it. No one believed it until recently, so I think the trend is just starting to turn the other way. With all the new books coming out and the rise of Christian lawyers who are arguing cases, I think we're going to see a turnaround on some of the injustices Christian students are facing on public school campuses.

Every person—including every Christian—has equal protection under the Constitution. That protection includes freedom of religion, freedom of speech, freedom of association, the right to hear, and the right to be treated equally under the law.

The Hardest Test at High School
LARRY RICHARDS

HIGH SCHOOL PRESENTS ALL SORTS OF PRESSURES THAT challenge a teen's values and faith. Most children are brought up thinking everyone is like them, more or less. Their childhood friends are selected from a closed neighborhood group that has the same values. The adults they know are chosen by their parents through association at church or other groups. Though they may be exposed to people with different values, their everyday life takes place among a homogeneous group that has a similar outlook on the world.

But when they get to high school, teens are confronted with a very different culture. Suddenly the teen's values are challenged. He meets kids from other neighborhoods. He sees teens who like to have fun in ways that are unacceptable to the Christian. He sees the Playboy philosophy at work. He becomes aware that there are other adults whom he respects, namely teachers, who have different values than his parents.

In light of these pressures and challenges, parents can expect young people to question their faith. Some parents think that questioning is a negative behavior, but it's not. Questioning and doubting are very natural and positive experiences. Developing personal convictions is part of the growth process, and one way to do that is by questioning.

In fact, if a young person doesn't question, he's likely to have more problems later on. He should question practices and beliefs that he took for granted when he was younger. He should wrestle with the basic foundation of his faith as well as the superficial issues of Christianity.

● *An open atmosphere.* To facilitate this, a teen needs an atmosphere at home where doubts and questions can be talked about, where he is free to raise issues without his parents assuming that his faith is on the verge of being destroyed. Providing that atmosphere is one key way parents can help a teen survive the pressures put on his spiritual life at school.

It's important, though, for parents to be careful not to contribute to the strain by putting pressure on the teen in the form of negative expectations. This can happen when parents communicate a lack of trust in the teen's ability to work through questions and make good choices. Panicky reactions like, "I'm scared to death you're going to go wrong" cause the teen to feel guilty and to wonder, "Am I trustworthy? Maybe I'm not."

A teen may come to his father and say, "Dad, today a couple of guys sitting outside school lit up a joint and asked me to do it, but I said no." If Dad becomes alarmed and flies off the handle, his son may decide it's not worth the risk to tell him the next time something like that happens. What's more, the boy may begin to doubt his ability to make a good choice.

Instead, parents need to respond and deal with their teen on the assumption that he is going to make the right decision. Parents can help him work through tough situations by asking questions like, "How did you react to that?" "What did you think?" "How are you going to handle that in the future?" By doing so, they're providing support that will help strengthen their teen's confidence in decision-making.

That's why I decided to send my oldest son to public high school. Up until then, he had gone to a Christian school. But I wanted him to face the kinds of choices a young person has to make while he was still at home so I could help him. I didn't want him to face those issues later when I wasn't around to listen and help.

● *Important support systems.* Teens also need support relationships with their peer group. This doesn't have to be a group of eighty kids; just one or two other teens who share his values are enough to give the teen encouragement and strength in handling the pressures.

Youth for Christ, Young Life, and Campus Crusade have significant ministries with kids in this area because they give teens a chance to meet other Christians at their school. This is especially important if the teen goes to a church where kids come from a large geographic area and don't go to the same high school.

My teenagers were fortunate to have close relationships with a few kids who shared their values while in high school. They had grown up in a certain value context and felt comfortable with others who shared those values. If I had jumped on their backs all the time at home, they might not have felt comfortable, and made different choices for friends as a reaction. But, while they did some crazy things, they never got into immoral or harmful kinds of behavior.

A relationship with an older person with whom to talk through his doubts and questions also bolsters a teen's faith. This doesn't have to be a parent; in fact it may be even better if he or she is a youth adviser, family friend, or Sunday School teacher— any adult with whom the teen feels comfortable and who can help explore troublesome issues in a nonjudgmental way.

Parents can't be at school with their teen to help him with all the challenges to his faith. But they can develop a healthy relationship and have good communication. They can provide an atmosphere where the teen is free to question. They can help him sort through his responses to tough situations and they can let their teen know they have confidence that he will make good decisions.

What Do You Do When Your Child Gets into a Bad Teaching Situation?
CLIFF SCHIMMELS

I VISIT ABOUT 200 CLASSROOMS A YEAR. SINCE I HAVE BEEN doing that for twelve years, I must know at least 600 or 700 teachers. Last year I visited classrooms in five different states. Only on very rare occasions do I see teaching methods or even content which concern me. Most of what I see is both sound and solid. In fact, most of the teachers I know want the same things for children as most parents want—to help the child through childhood and adolescence and into adulthood as a thinking, courteous, moral human being. Most of the disagreements between teachers and parents are about methods of getting there and not about the ultimate outcome.

When I do see bad teaching, it is usually because of laziness rather than resolution. A teacher is just looking for an easier or quicker way of doing something and gets caught up in a bad practice or using an approach which is questionable.

In fact, I am actually rather impressed with most teachers' commitments to their tasks. A junior high school asked me to speak to their teachers after school. Nearly two thirds of the staff voluntarily stayed three hours after class to hear material which they hoped would help them do their jobs better. I went to another school a full hour before school, and three fourths of the teachers voluntarily came to a training session. Of course, not all teachers are that committed, but I am still impressed with those numbers.

But now that I have convinced you that teachers are a pretty good lot and school is a happy place, your child will probably get the one who is lazy or indifferent or wants to take advantage of his position with bizarre material, strange opinions, or disturbing teaching methods. As long as there are some like that, there is always a possibility that your child may get one. In that case, you need to be prepared to take positive action to ensure that your child's education is not marred by an encounter with a bad teacher, or even a bad curriculum decision. Let me suggest a course of action.

1. *Establish and maintain a working relationship with your child.* I know that sounds a little silly, but it is the beginning to your child's educational success. Maintain a close enough relationship with your child to have some idea what he is learning, how he is being taught, and what is disturbing him. Frankly, I am not impressed with parents who attend open house in November and are shocked to discover what their child is learning. If you don't have a closer relationship than that, there is a bigger problem at home than at school.

Listen to your child talk during those special times when the family is at ease together, such as mealtimes. If your family doesn't have any of those times, establish them. Make sure you are the kind of adult your child can come to with his thoughts, ideas, and frustrations. Respect him as a human being. Don't be aloof or overly protective, reacting to every minor experience your child encounters.

With this kind of relationship with your child, you will know immediately when something happens which bothers him or you. You will be able to assess both the extent and the urgency of the problem, and you will be able to take whatever action you feel will best help your child.

Also, by having that kind of relationship with your child, you can help your child turn the facts he learns into positive learning experiences. For example, I appreciate a good teacher teaching my child information. When my son was in high school, one teacher taught him about Communism. I am pleased that he learned that information, but it is my responsibility to make sure my son isn't a Communist. Now that my son knows the basic facts, I need to complete the lesson at home.

2. *Establish and maintain a working relationship with the school and the classroom teacher.* Since your child spends so many hours in school, get to know the people who are working with him. Begin early. Establish a friendly relationship. Visit the teacher and get to know him on a personal basis. If you catch the teacher doing something right, send him a note thanking him. Let the teacher know *you* on a personal basis. That way the teacher will know your convictions and motivations, and this alone may cause the teacher to rethink some of his actions if you ever need to discuss a matter of concern with him. Always

remember that you and that teacher are partners in this business of rearing your child.

If a problem develops, first go straight to the source. If you have a problem with the teacher, go see the teacher. If you aren't satisfied, then go to the superiors. Don't go when you are angry.

Hear the other side. State your side. See if you can reach an agreement. If you can't, then insist that your child be excused from whatever activity you find unsatisfactory. Both common sense and the courts say that no child has to participate in any classroom activity which is offensive to his faith.

3. *Learn how the system works.* If you wish to take an unsatisfactory situation further than your own house, you need to know something about how the system works.

In theory, at least, your public school is primarily a local institution functioning on decisions made by your neighbors, assembled together on a school board. If you don't agree with the decisions those neighbors make, go to a meeting and tell them. If that board doesn't respond, then get on the board yourself. The pay is lousy, but the work is vital.

If the unsatisfactory decision or course of action is at the state level, find out how that system works and make sure people in charge know how you feel. You may need to write a few letters, make a few telephone calls, or even travel a bit, but you *can* have an influence. Just make sure you have done your homework and that you know what you are talking about. If the effort seems too much, perhaps you should rethink the significance of your complaint.

Consider Mel and Norma Gabler of Texas. A few years ago, they decided they didn't like what was in their children's textbooks, so they chose to do something about it. They learned how the textbook adoption system works in Texas, and they went to work through the system. They studied hard; they prepared their arguments well; and they have had a profound effect on what is published in school textbooks not only in Texas but throughout the nation.

If we don't learn anything else from the Gablers, we should at least learn that the system still listens to people.

Should We Allow Our Child to Take a Public-School Sex Education Course?

MARK COSGROVE

TO THE BEST OF THEIR ABILITY, CHRISTIAN PARENTS SHOULD already be giving their children sex education at home. Most often, sex education courses are offered late in the child's elementary school training, perhaps not until high school. And if you have any doubts about the quality or value of the school's sex education program, you can counteract its possible bad effects by giving your child sound Christian training in the meaning of sexuality.

Realize that your child will get unchristian teaching about sex from a variety of sources—for example, from conversations with friends, from books and magazines, and from TV. So even if you do not allow your child to attend a sex education course at school, he will receive sex education in other ways. You must be sure that your child is getting a Christ-centered understanding of sexuality.

There are several specific things you may do to assess the value of your school's sex education program. Most schools are quite eager to have their parents' support before any criticism or problem arises, so they want you to be well-informed about what they are doing. You could say to your school principal or the appropriate teacher, "I hear that a sex education course is being offered, and my child is interested in taking it. May I sit in on the class?" If that is not permitted, you could ask, "May I see the instructional materials that will be used?" That is a far more effective way to ensure that your child receives sound instruction than waiting to ask questions after your child has begun the course. If you try to challenge the content of the course then— with either the individual teacher, the principal, or the school board—you will not be likely to effect constructive changes. This is why most public schools want parents to make full inquiry about such courses before their children enroll.

If the sex education course is required, you should likewise be aware of what is being taught so that you can supplement the course with clear Christian teaching at home. Sit in on some class sessions; examine the course materials; talk with the teacher about the course plan. In every way, try to gain an overview of what the class will be doing.

Here are several subjects that may be taught in a public-school sex education course in ways that conflict with your Christian values. Give special attention to the course's emphasis on:

Premarital sex. Does the course recommend or condone premarital intercourse? Does it assume that many students will engage in premarital sex? You should communicate to your child that premarital sexual relations are *not* the norm for Christian young people.

Abortion. Most public school studies on human sexuality try to take a neutral stance on this issue. But the way the textbooks are written or the films are edited may imply that abortion is a logical option for a pregnant girl.

Homosexuality. While homosexuality is neither praised nor condemned in most public-school courses on sexuality, it may be presented in a way that suggests that it too is a reasonable option for a young person.

These three issues are bound to arise in any meaningful discussion of human sexuality. In addition, every compassionate Christian young person must ask, "What are our responsibilities to the unwed mother? to the illegitimate child? to the victim of AIDS?" We cannot hope to ignore these questions or shield our children from them. Our concern as Christian parents, however, is to be sure that our children can deal with them within a Christian framework. Your child may never be tempted to get involved in any of these activities, but many young people will. And when your child sees his peers experimenting with these "alternate lifestyles," he will need a clear rationale for living as a Christian does.

Our children should learn to understand the situation of those who are entangled in sexual problems. People who are in their throes can be redeemed through the power of Jesus Christ. So I hope that, in our efforts to warn our children of these perversions of God's plan for sex, we do not give them a revulsion for the people who are immersed in them. Our children should be well informed yet compassionate about sexual problems.

When you visit your Christian bookstore, look for material that you can use to teach your children Christian values about sexuality. Ask your pastor or Christian bookseller to recommend books that will help you teach your child a wholesome view of sexuality. I know it's not always easy to find good teaching aids. But I believe our goal of teaching children how to be mature, responsible, and Christ-honoring adults is well worth the effort of finding the best resources to train them, in the school and in the home.

CHAPTER
8

How Do I Help
My Child Get Along
with Others?

How Do Children Learn to Share?
BYRON EMMERT

MY THREE-YEAR-OLD SON, TYLER, IS SITTING ON THE floor taking inventory of the sweet haul he made during the recent Halloween trick-or-treating ritual. Across from him sits Amy, another three-year-old, who is visiting.

Tyler knows his quota is one, so he carefully surveys his treasure and selectively plops a caramel into his mouth with a big grin. Meanwhile, with her inventory stockpiled at home, Amy drools with pleading eyes.

"Tyler, wouldn't you like to share a piece of candy with Amy?" I suggest. Tyler slowly turns his head back and forth to let me know that no, he would not like to give up any of his candy.

Wanting to be nice to our visitor, and believing this to be a good time to teach my son about sharing, I reason, "Do you think it's fair that you have candy to eat while Amy doesn't? Why don't you be nice and give her a piece of candy?"

Tyler's response is to move his plastic pumpkin full of candy behind his back, where he can protect it.

Now I become more insistent. "Tyler, how would you feel if you were at Amy's house and she didn't share her candy with you? You wouldn't like it, would you? So, you'd better share!"

Tyler really gets stubborn now and guards his bucket of sweets with both arms as he shakes his whole body, which translates, "No way!"

My fatherly patience has had it. I use my last resort. "Tyler, you give a piece of candy to Amy, or I'll spank you!"

Finding this mandate to be quite persuasive, Tyler pushes his pail of goodies toward Amy and says, "Don't take a big piece."

Is it possible to teach values to a three-year-old? How can children learn how to share?

It may be helpful to remember that the Bible consistently teaches that a child is born with a sinful nature (Ps. 51:5; Rom. 5:12). This explains a child's basic tendency to be selfish.

Children usually view choices in terms of their physical or pleasurable consequences. If a child is rewarded for something, it is good. If he is punished for something, it is bad. He is not concerned about his decisions affecting others. What's important is how it affects his own desires and self-centered needs. In Tyler's thinking, this meant that being selfish was good for him because he could have all the candy for himself. Being selfish became bad for him when he realized that the spanking would bring him more pain than the pleasure of one more piece of candy. This does not mean that spanking is the key to teaching children how to share, although in certain situations it is a wonderful influence. It does mean we must help our children learn how to share at their level of thinking. "He who spares the rod hates his son, but he who loves him is careful to discipline him" (Prov. 13:24, NIV).

Good discipline includes instruction. Depending on the age-and reasoning-levels of our children, here are some ideas to consider as we lovingly instruct them how to share:

1. *Be an example of sharing.* This is probably the most important. Children will imitate the values of those they admire. As parents, if we don't model sharing attitudes and actions in and out of the home, we can't expect our children to share. Whether it be a treat, a task, or part of our time, sharing must start with us.

2. *Share by taking turns.* A candy bar can be divided equally

and enjoyed by more than one child at the same time. A toy truck cannot. Kids need to learn that sharing sometimes means waiting. A good way to do this is to set a watch or a timer and switch the coveted toy between children every five minutes. Often, children will begin to share naturally once they experience this system of taking turns.

3. *Pray about sharing.* We can help our children pray to God to help them share and for forgiveness when they don't. As a result, they will begin to learn that sharing pleases God and this will help influence their actions.

4. *Read about sharing.* There are many Bible stories and children's books that illustrate sharing. Children love stories about other children. A local Christian bookstore will be a great help.

5. *Talk about sharing.* Whenever the opportunity presents itself, we must take advantage of those teachable moments when we and our children see someone being a good or bad example of sharing. This might be a real situation at home or at play, a conversation following Sunday School or school, or a TV program like "Sesame Street."

6. *Play games that teach sharing.* There are many children's games that deal with the subject of sharing. Check with a Christian bookstore or make up your own.

7. *Do sharing projects.* Involve your whole family in a project that requires giving something to someone else. For example, every family member could come up with a toy or some clothing to give to a needy family. Tell your children about the idea and let them brainstorm different projects.

8. *Take pictures of sharing.* Pick a day or a weekend and keep your camera ready to capture those moments when someone in your family is sharing with someone else. Periodically look at the pictures together and ask your children to remember how they shared and how it made them feel.

9. *Compliment your children's sharing.* Children will likely repeat an action if they receive positive reinforcement. We must praise them and encourage them with words, hugs, or rewards whenever they share. If we give our kids positive strokes, they'll mind; if we don't, they'll need more on the behind.

10. *Discipline children when they don't share.* Until a child can understand that it is right to share, he needs to experience

bad consequences for being selfish. A spanking or the removal of a favorite toy will encourage a child to behave less selfishly. If the discipline is consistent, the child will eventually get the message.

Quarreling
PAUL & VIRGINIA NURMI

QUARRELING IS A PART OF LIFE, WHETHER WE CALL IT debating, arguing, or a difference of opinion.

Certain situations and circumstances naturally promote more quarrels than others. In our house we know that suppertime is the most quarrel-prone time of our day. Also, any time the daily family routine is upset creates an environment that is quarrel-prone, even if this change in routine is positive (e.g., a vacation or holiday). A wise parent is aware of the pattern, can calm the tensions that inevitably arise, and make quarreling as tolerable and constructive as possible.

Quarreling among children comes in two degrees: the insignificant and the serious. A quick analysis of what is brewing will show parents how to bring about a fast resolution. For the less-than-fluent toddler, emotional flare-ups are the result of misunderstanding or the inability to communicate. Teaching our children to say, "Please," is a giant step toward positive communication and away from fussing.

When older kids have insignificant quarrels it is often better to let them work out these squabbles themselves. This approach cuts down on the tattletale syndrome and is a valuable learning situation. Kids need to learn how to take responsibility for their own disagreements. A simple, "You'll have to work it out for yourselves" and a calm closing of the door often throws cold water on a formerly heated struggle.

Some circumstances qualify as serious quarrels. These out-of-hand incidents might result in bodily harm and call for direct intervention.

It is hard not to jump to conclusions, but things are not always as they seem. Now is the teachable moment to encourage the quarreling skills that can be beneficial to your child for the rest

SHARING VS. TURN-TAKING

"Why don't kids share their toys?" we wonder. Perhaps one reason is the use of the word *share*. Children have learned that to *share* means to "give part of something to someone else." Mom and Dad have told them to "share" their candy with their friends and to "share" their dessert with their brothers and sisters. They have also heard about how God "shares" His love, and they have seen us "share" our money and food with them.

They resist, therefore, when told to "share" a favorite toy with a friend. You can't split a truck or a doll. Of course, we really mean that they should share the playing time, but this usually is not communicated.

An easy solution is to tell them to "take turns" instead of to "share." Taking turns with a toy means that a person has the exclusive use of it for a certain time.

Yes, children are selfish; but their resistance to sharing may just be a problem with words. Use "taking turns" instead and clear up the confusion.

YFC Editors

of his life. If emotions are running too high, a period of separation and cool-down is the first step. Not much can be accomplished when a child is so upset that he cannot get the words out. When everyone is emotionally controlled, each should tell his side of the story. The stories must be told without name-calling or verbal cutdowns. Using exaggerations or assuming the other person's motives is not allowed. In other words, the story must be told in first person. This is the chance to express legitimate feelings. A calm, benevolent mediator can then hand down the verdict.

What kind of verdict? Just as there are two sides to every story, there are usually two people at fault in every quarrel. Most often it boils down to selfishness. This is the opportune time to give the "there are more people in this family than just you" speech. Living together enjoyably requires a lot of give and take on everyone's part. It is a lesson best begun at an early age. An "I am sorry" and a hug or smile go a long way toward mending ruffled emotions and relationships. What if one child doesn't feel sorry? An apology does not have to come from the emotion of being sorry. The appropriate action needs to be taken; and usually the feeling will come later.

If quarreling is inevitable, can we do anything to prevent it? When our first son was in kindergarten, he learned Bible verses for each letter of the alphabet. The "H" verse was: "How good and pleasant it is when brothers live together in unity!" (Ps. 133:1) That came in very handy as quarrels began to erupt. A quick, "Do you remember our 'H' verse?" brought a sly smile and a cooling of heated emotions.

But probably the best preventative medicine comes before quarrels even begin. Spend time telling each of the kids how much the other siblings love them and point out positive acts among siblings. That may sound contrived, but it works beautifully.

How to Help Your Child Choose Good Friends
CHARLES SWINDOLL

ONE OF THE MAJOR CONTRIBUTIONS PARENTS CAN MAKE to a child is helping him learn to choose good friends.

We began when our children were very young and teachable. We pointed out the good qualities of our friends. And our children learned by seeing us interact with our friends how important they were to us.

We tried to get them to think about the type of people they wanted to spend their time with—people who would strengthen them morally, people with good self-esteem. We stressed the advantage of finding friends with good parents and homes with high ideals.

I remember when one of our daughters chose a friend who wasn't good for her. She's a sensitive girl and was easily swayed in her early years. We sat her down one day and just talked about her friend—what her home life was like, and what the characteristics of her family seemed to be. Then we asked our daughter what things she liked in our home and what was important to her. I asked her to think about the parallels between her life and the life she wanted, and that of her new friend. As I suspected, she couldn't think of too many. By realizing that there was such a marked contrast between her life and ideals and those of her new friend, our daughter began to see things in a new light.

As I mentioned before, begin in the early years, when your child is very teachable—when he's listening and sensitive. When we let our daughter think through her new choice, she was sensitive and open to our counsel.

My daughter realized that the characteristics of her friend's home could very easily carry over into her own life. Unfortunately, when the neighbor child grew into the teen years, she mirrored the negative characteristics of her environment. One night at the dinner table, my daughter said, "Remember our talk way back about so-and-so? I'm so glad that I chose against making her a close friend."

A second point is that we've got to be careful that we don't overkill. Sometimes when parents make the decision *for* their teen, giving him no option, the teen is provoked to rebel and become an intimate companion of the person the parents disapprove of. If teens feel that they can be friends with only three people that the whole family agrees on, they can be pushed to this extreme.

A related problem in Christian homes is helping teens see the distinction between avoiding friendships with backsliders and not becoming judgmental of non-Christians. The latter portion of 1 Corinthians 5 speaks about our associations with others. As parents, we must be careful not to instill a pious "holier-than-thou" attitude with our teens. Christ was compassionate with unbelievers. Our teens need to know how to be compassionate without lowering their standards.

Friends are a very tricky but very important area in which parents need to instruct teens. Start as soon as possible and be a role model by wisely choosing your own friends.

The Power of Peer Pressure
BARRY ST. CLAIR

THE NUMBER ONE REASON TEENS GIVE IN TO PEER PRESsure is a bad self-image. A teen who has low self-esteem feels a strong need to have others agree with him. To him, this means that he's made a good decision. But this need often causes a teen to be unable to respect or accept others as they are. Therefore, he is more susceptible to negative peer pressure.

The effect of giving in to peer pressure is what sociologist David Reisman calls an "other-directed personality." The teen develops a sixth sense which enables him to feel out what others expect of him and then act accordingly. In other words, a teen will compromise his own identity in order to be accepted by his peers.

The second major cause for giving in to peer pressure is fear. Fear keeps teenagers from being their own unique selves and usually expresses itself in several ways. A teen may fear what his friends will think of him. As a result, most teenagers try to build relationships and solidify their reputations without offending anyone.

Fear also expresses itself when a teenager is scared that choosing to follow God won't be any fun.

And lastly, in what I call the "Chameleon Process," a teen, afraid of losing friendships, will develop the knack of blending in when he's with his friends because he's too self-conscious to stand up for what he believes. Proverbs 18:24 says, "A man of many friends comes to ruin, but there is a friend who sticks closer than a brother" (NASB). Second Timothy 1:7 also speaks to the issue of fear: "For God has not given us a spirit of timidity, but of power and love and discipline" (NASB).

Parents need to respond to the powerful force of peer pressure in several ways. First, they must realize the depth of the problem. During the teen years, the most important area in their child's life is that of acceptance. Risking rejection by his friends (which could involve being badly hurt) is a daily danger for a teenager. [*continued on p. 111*]

WHEN YOUNG PEOPLE
"KEEP UP WITH THE JONESES"

In a recent television program, a group of teenagers was asked, "What do you see as the greatest problem facing teens today?" Overwhelmingly, the response was, "Peer pressure."

Peer pressure affects all teenagers in some way. And it isn't all bad. Peer pressure causes us to behave according to standards set by a group. These standards may be good, poor, or self-destructive.

We tend to think of peer pressure only as a negative force for children and teenagers. But many young people have been challenged to excel in schoolwork or in sports because of healthy competition. Often a young person learns the value of money when he must save his allowance to buy something that "everyone" has.

Peer pressure is not a problem experienced just by teenagers. As adults, we call it "keeping up with the Joneses." We are still conforming to standards set by someone else. But maturity allows us to be less influenced by others.

Being accepted by others—our family, classmates, or coworkers—helps us develop positive self-images. That, in turn, gives us the character to withstand temporary failure, rejection, or loneliness. Being part of a group provides affirmation. And when the group has healthy standards, the peer pressure is a positive force.

But as parents, we often see young people influenced by negative peer pressure. Following the crowd has led many teens into drugs, sexual experimentation, cheating, etc. Teens and preteens are too often wrongly influenced by others before they've established their own standards and values.

How can we help?

First, *accept peer pressure as normal.* Everyone experiences it—young children, teens, and adults. It's a necessary part of society, since some conformity to rules and guidelines is vital if we're to survive. (Imagine if we all drove as fast as we wanted!)

Second, *give positive support.* Praise young people when they achieve. Don't wait until your teen earns straight A's, pitches a no-hitter, or plays like a concert pianist. Encouragement strengthens identity.

Third, *examine yourself.* The old adage, "Do as I say, not as I do," seldom works with teens. As they are stretching, trying to find their own limits, teenagers need to see examples of mature adults with healthy values and Christian lifestyles.

Finally, *give teens as much choice as they can handle, within clearly defined guidelines.* For example, "John, today I'd like you to mow the lawn. You can do it anytime, as long as it's done by suppertime." As a young person gets more practice making decisions—and facing the consequences of his decision-making—he becomes more confident of taking control. A young person who has planned his own schedule for doing homework will be more confident when he must decide whether or not he should join the group for an after-school snack.

The secret is giving up control gradually. Never releasing control forces teens to rebel. And dropping all controls overnight is like putting a ship in the middle of the ocean without a rudder, map, or compass.

Though it often seems children (and especially teenagers) don't want to receive guidance and rules from adults, that isn't true. The controls and guidelines tell a child that someone cares. While they may not like all the rules, interviews with young people show that they'd rather have too many rules than none at all.

We must pass our traditions, wisdom, beliefs, and convictions on to our children. Teens need positive models for growth—emotionally, physically, and spiritually. Values deeply planted in our children help them resist the quick cure—drugs, drinking, sex—for too much negative peer pressure.

YFC Editors

Second, parents need to understand the fact that being accepted by friends is more important to their teen than being accepted by parents. Most teenagers do *not* want to conform to the lifestyles and actions of their peers. They want to stand on their own, but in most cases they lack the self-respect and confidence to resist peer pressure.

The parents' primary responsibility in helping their teen deal with negative peer pressure is to provide an atmosphere, such as a church youth group, where their teen can find acceptance with Christian peers. Though they can't totally remedy the situation, parents *can* express concern and keep the lines of communication open. Sharing their own experiences and frustrations with peer pressure can be an encouragement to a struggling son or daughter.

By developing their child's self-image and convictions, parents can help him better cope with peer pressure.

Self-image

God expects His children to have good self-images as seen in Mark 12:31, Christ's commandment "to love your neighbor as yourself." In Psalm 139:13-16, we are told that no one else is like us—that we are fearfully and wonderfully made. God created your child for a unique purpose, and He intends to fulfill that purpose.

Parents need to develop their teen's self-image in three areas: mental, physical, and spiritual. In the mental and physical realms, they can encourage their teenager to accept his capabilities, such as athletic ability, natural intelligence, and inborn musical talents, right where they are—while working to improve those areas that show promise. Don't allow a teen to limit his self-image to physical appearance or abilities. Though compliments on looks and achievements are very important to a teenager, 1 Samuel 16:7 assures us that God looks on the heart. He is more concerned with inner beauty than He is with what we look like on the outside.

Spiritually, a teen needs to realize that his relationship to God has potential for change and growth. He also needs to know that he can rely on his parents to always be there in his time of need. That's God's way of loving kids! Parents should encourage their teen and pray specifically for him and his friends.

Convictions

Developing positive convictions in a teen can help him deal with negative peer pressure. A teenager who has no convictions will fit in with any group of people. That's a sign of real immaturity. On the other hand, a teen who can stand up and say, "Hey, I'm doing that for these reasons . . . " shows a real maturity.

Convictions must come from the teen's own experiences and study—not from another person. The only solid convictions come from the Word of God. I like to use the comparison between a thermometer and a thermostat. The thermometer is an instrument that is *controlled* by the environment; the thermostat is an instrument that *controls* the environment. In their ability to develop convictions, teens can be either thermometers or thermostats.

Standing up for convictions will result in conflict, not conformity. Teens must be aware that they are going to run into conflict with their friends as they develop convictions, yet by having convictions, teens are rewarded by developing self-respect and maturity.

The first step toward helping your teen develop convictions is to help him analyze his relationships with others. Are his friends really interested in him? Is God really interested in him? What are his friends' responses when he crosses them?

The second step is to help your teen choose to go God's way. First John 2:15-17 talks about the importance of remaining in God's will. Your teen needs to learn that it takes a conscious decision to walk God's way.

The third step is to encourage your teen to allow God to overcome fear. Perfect love casts out fear of rejection.

A final step is to help your teen *verbally* identify with Jesus Christ. To say, "Well, because my mom won't let me," or "I'm not going to buy a six-pack because I'm not thirsty" is a cop-out. I suggest using the statement, "Because I belong to Jesus Christ, I can do this or I can't do that." That kind of statement clarifies where he stands.

Of course, the most significant way to deal with peer pressure is to remedy the situation while your child is still young. If parents wait until their child is sixteen to start developing convictions or building up his self-image, it's possibly too late. By helping their child develop solid convictions and overcome the

112

fear of rejection, parents can be confident that their teenager will grow into a "thermostat" in control of his environment.

ENCOURAGING CHRISTIAN FELLOWSHIP

How can you help your teens' spiritual development and get them involved with other Christian teens?

1. Start going to church with your family when your children are very young. Go to Sunday School and have your children attend a class too. Get into the habit of family worship right from the start (or right now, if you haven't already!). Then speak well of your church and its activities; don't criticize the church all week, then expect your kids to want to be there every Sunday or wonder ·why they don't like the youth leader.

2. Find out what your church youth group does— don't assume it's effective (especially if your kids have gone and not liked it). Find out what's happening. And don't let yourself think that your parental role is threatened by youth leaders—they can help; they're not competing with you. Support them. If your teen would rather talk to them than you and *does*, accept that at this point in your child's life and make efforts to improve listening and communication at home.

3. Be willing to take your kids (and their friends at times too) to the church-sponsored activities.

4. Look into options for your teens (other churches, for example).

5. If nothing is available, take the initiative to get something going. Seek out resources. Be willing to help. Get other teens' parents interested and involved.

6. Give your kids a choice—don't cram certain friends or even Christian fellowship down their throats. Respect their choice of friends while encouraging Christian contacts.

YFC Editors

Unsuitable Friends
DAVID & GAIL VEERMAN

THERE IS NOTHING QUITE SO REFRESHING AS THE INNO-
cence of a child, overflowing with wonder, trust, and naiveté.
And there is nothing quite so devastating as the loss of that
innocence. But babies become toddlers who become little kids
who become "young ladies and gentlemen" who become
teenagers. . . .

Along the way, they learn from media, teachers, books, friends,
and others who help them grow up, who expose them to the
"real world." As much as we would like to shelter our children,
we know we must help them to mature, to be ready to live in
society.

One of the most difficult areas with which to deal is friendships. We want our children to have friends, but what do we do
if they choose friends whom we think are unsuitable? Immediately, we want to shelter and protect them. These kids are bad
influences, we think, and we don't want them around. But instead of overreacting, nagging, or outright prohibiting any contact with the unwanted friend, answer these important questions:

What makes the child unsuitable? Are you reacting to the
way she looks? Do you exclude him because of your personal
prejudices and biases? Or are there valid grounds for concern?

Try to identify the unsuitable traits. Possibilities could include
the following: uses bad language, has bad habits, is a troublemak-
er, shows disrespect for parents and other adults, misuses others'
property, encourages others to do wrong. Any one of these is
cause for concern.

After this analysis, ask *why* this child behaves this way. Perhaps
there is a difficult home situation. Maybe he is seeking attention
or love. Maybe she is covering a deep hurt. Then pray for the
child. You may be able to help him or her through your acceptance, guidance, and love.

Why is your child drawn to that child? It may be that *your*
child has emotional struggles or needs that aren't being met at
home. The friendship can be a clue to what is going on in her

life. Opposites attract, says the proverb, but then birds of a feather flock together. Is it possible that the unsuitable friend is reflecting heretofore hidden traits of your youngster? On the other hand, your child may be motivated by concern for the other person. Perhaps she is trying to reach out to her, to be a help.

GETTING OUT OF THE BAD CROWD

When a child goes to school, particularly in our society where the schools are very large, she will find a variety of peer groups. For example, the kid who is a marijuana user will find a group of people in the same boat and will gravitate toward them. So the parents decide to pull her out of the school and put her in a Christian high school. But even at a Christian high school, some kids are into drugs, and each child will gravitate to the group that embodies her values.

This is true in grade school, in junior high, and all the way through: a child will seek out the group that tends to reflect who she is.

One good solution to this problem is for parents to become involved in some positive youth program with their children. They can endeavor to create an environment in which Christian values can survive—such as Campus Life or Young Life clubs. If parents can't separate the child from the group, the only alternative is to do everything possible to transform the group.

Tony Campolo

The answers to these two questions will determine your next steps. Choose a combination of the following:

1. *Involve the friend in your home.* If his home is the source of the bad influence, try to bring him into your house. This will allow you to get to know him, and he will be able to see your Christian love in action. Take the initiative and invite him to go with you to the game or the park. This will also help your child see the contrast in families and appreciate what he has at home.

2. *Look for teaching opportunities.* Without being judgmental, carefully (and quietly) talk to your child about your values and how they compare to her friend's. Then let her draw the conclusions—don't jump in with the lesson for the day. An excellent time for this would be when your child tells you something her friend got in trouble for or something the other family is doing. Remember that this teaching is not always focused on the friend's needs. Ask why your child feels as she does, and try to discover her hidden needs as well.

3. *Provide opportunities for your child to be with other kids.* There are many clubs, trips, lessons, teams, and other activities sponsored by church, school, park district, and other organizations. By involving your child in some of these, you will help him meet other children and probably make new friends. How much free time does he have after school? There are many extracurricular possibilities. Or you may try interesting him in a hobby, especially one you can work on together. These new activities may not pull your child away from the undesirable friend, but they will open up possibilities for new, positive friendships to develop.

4. *Pray and be patient.* Unless this is a very destructive relationship where, after careful consideration and consultation, a forced separation must be made, chances are great that your child will grow past this person or stage. Don't make such an effort to win the battle that you lose the war.

This is a parenting situation that must be handled with care. So many of your needs are mixed with your child's, and you will be tempted to react impulsively. But working through friendships together can be a tremendous learning and growing experience for both of you. Don't miss it.

Raising Good Children in a "Bad" Neighborhood
HARVEY HOOK

A COMMON QUESTION FOR TODAY'S FAMILY IS HOW TO provide the very best environment for your children while living within your means. This can often mean apartments, substandard housing, and unsafe streets. Rita and I find ourselves in this very situation with our first child. We are in a high-crime, low-income neighborhood of limited resources—far from many of our friends. However, we have discovered several principles that have led to a most successful story. The following adjustments have proven to meet our child-raising needs:

First, *accept the given limitations of your present circumstances.* It might not be what you want but it is what you have. Start there and make the best of it. This simple but most significant act is vital to family health. This allows you to be creative in responding to many child-raising needs.

Second, *build a network of friendships and relationships throughout your immediate community.* Become a part of your neighborhood and take ownership in it. Relationships will help you feel at home, create opportunities to share common concerns with others, and provide a much-needed support group. Should a special need or emergency arise, you will have a ready resource of people to respond. Part of this process is opening your home to others. Make your home "the place to be" for neighborhood children. This is especially important if you are concerned for your child's safety or supervision in other homes. Your love and influence will have an opportunity to touch the lives of many. In addition, as you are developing relationships with parents of other children, you will be able to assist in choosing the friends who will interact with and influence your child.

Third, *avail yourself of nearby or outside resources.* It only takes a few phone calls to locate the nearest or best-suited swimming pool, YMCA, library, park, or recreation center. Discover where they are located, hours and days they are open, supervision provided, and then *use* them!

Fourth, *take precautions to teach your children about any potential dangers they face in the neighborhood.* Issues such as traffic, unsafe streets, strangers, older teens, and where and when to play should be addressed in a straightforward manner. This will result in your children being trained and cautious but not fearful and insecure; in other words, they'll be well equipped to respond to their environment.

Last, *make your home comfortable, attractive, and warm.*

This can be done fairly inexpensively with paint, wallpaper, stenciling, etc. Let it reflect your tastes and personality. The attitude you project about your home will overflow to your entire family and will instill in them a sense of belonging.

By initiating these five principles, you are best able and most suited to meet the needs and demands you face in raising your children. Other issues such as a local church or schooling needs will also arise. However, these too can be resolved as resources are investigated and developed through relationships and community contacts. Volunteer to help at your child's school by tutoring or assisting in some manner. Bring your resources and abilities into play. Your influence will only add to the schooling experience. Should you attend a church in the neighborhood, ask to teach or to assist. There is always a need for concerned parents to provide leadership and role models for young children.

As I shared earlier, Rita and I, like so many others, find ourselves in a neighborhood that is not a good place to raise children. However, we have made the best of it and the situation is working. We have opened our lives and our home; we have applied these principles, and we have been blessed beyond measure.

CHAPTER 9

How Do I Help My Child Live for Jesus?

Living Faith
LARRY RICHARDS

MOSES LIVED AMONG PEOPLE WHO HAD SEEN GOD ACT. He told those people to communicate their faith and God's miracles to the next generation, which wasn't going to have miraculous experiences to back up their faith in God. They weren't going to have manna every morning; they weren't going to see the pillar of cloud and fire.

To help in this communication, Moses set down a very simple pattern for teaching faith (Deut. 6). First, the communicators—the adults—must love God. Parents can't teach a faith they don't possess. But if they are growing in their own relationship with God, taking His Word into their hearts, then they can't help communicating it!

Second, parents must be models of the faith they wish to teach. Moses said to teach God's Law "when you sit at home and when you walk along the road, when you lie down and when you get up" (Deut. 6:7, NIV). How can they do that? Through

SPIRITUAL GOALS FOR YOUR CHILDREN

Exactly what should you be trying to do for your children spiritually? Here are some goals you might have:

- They will believe in Jesus Christ as Saviour and Lord and have a personal relationship with Him.
- They will know the Bible and submit to its authority.
- They will pray regularly and see God answer prayer.
- They will live holy lives of obedience to God's Word, lives marked by love for and service to others.
- They will tell their friends about Jesus Christ.
- They will become active members of a local church.
- They will worship and praise God as a routine of life.

To accomplish these goals, you have at least three methods at your disposal. All three are described in the classic passage to fathers, Deuteronomy 6:4-9.

The first method is *personal example.* This is implied in verses 5-6, in which men are commanded to love God and have the Word of God planted in their hearts. Fathers who live this way show their children the way of the Lord in "living color."

The second method is *formal instruction.* This is implied in the first part of verse 7: "You shall teach them diligently to your sons" (NASB). There are many ways to teach God's Word to your children, but you, the parent, must do it, and you must do it with planning and perseverance.

The third method, seen in the last part of verse 7, is *informal teaching:* "When you sit at home and when you walk along the road, when you lie down and when you get up." All the normal living experiences of the day offer opportunities to teach if you take advantage of them.

Paul Heidebrecht

shared experiences. As adults go about their daily lives, questions come up. As they explain their actions, choices, values, and attitudes, they relate their lives to the Word of God.

We have a tendency to separate living and teaching faith, whereas the Bible intertwines them. Bible stories are important, but it is far more important to talk about the Bible through our lives. It is critically important to live our faith before our children.

It is helpful for parents to reflect on why they do what they do—to understand the reasons for their actions so they can explain them. Peter wrote, "Always be prepared to give an answer to everyone who asks you to give the reason for the hope that you have" (1 Peter 3:15, NIV). The reason does not have to be theological; children usually prefer simple explanations anyway.

I grew up during the Depression years. We didn't have a lot of money. My dad was a rural mail carrier, and I knew we weren't loaded. Yet I can remember a drawer in which Mom and Dad kept the church money—and there was always a lot. At times I'd ask what the money was for. Mom would talk about the missionaries it would help support. She explained that she and Dad wanted to give to those who depended on people like them for their income. Just observing their faith in action in that way made a lasting impression on me.

Understanding Your Child's Spiritual Development
PAUL HEIDEBRECHT

AS CHRISTIAN PARENTS, WE WANT OUR CHILDREN TO BElieve in Jesus Christ as Saviour and Lord and to have a personal relationship with Him. But we cannot give our adult faith directly to our small children because they are not yet ready for it. Spiritual development—like physical, emotional, and intellectual development—is a gradual process with definite stages.

We can most effectively guide our children to Jesus if we understand how the stages of spiritual development work.

● *Infancy.* This is the age of beginnings. Spiritual learning begins here, before your child can walk, talk, or even sit up. If she is to be emotionally healthy, your child must know first of all that you love her. The feeling of being loved will also provide the foundation for her understanding of the biblical truth that God loves her.

As an infant, your child can learn what it means to trust. If she can trust her parents for her basic needs, she will someday also be able to trust God for her spiritual needs. Your ability to show your child gentleness, love, patience, and firmness may determine how she responds to God later in life.

● *Ages 2-3.* Your child believes most of what he hears, and he will certainly be open to spiritual truths. Because you converse with him in words, you can introduce some simple but significant spiritual truths.

He cannot understand symbols such as the "lost sheep" or the "bread of life." Nor can he understand spiritual concepts such as man's sinful nature, the Trinity, or that Jesus is both God and man. However, he will understand such concepts as love, trust, forgiveness, and the consequences of sinful actions—if they are related to everyday experiences with which he is familiar.

Your child can know that God is the Creator and that He is all-powerful, perfect, and our provider. He can know that God is a real person who loves and cares about him, even when he is bad. Your child can begin to say his own prayers when he is about three years old. He can begin to express his own love for God the Father and Jesus.

Your child can identify with Jesus as a real person and as Someone who wants to be his best friend. He can know that Jesus is loving and caring and that He came to earth a very long time ago as a baby, grew up as a boy, and became a man. He can know that Jesus died on the cross, though he will not understand all the implications, and he can know that Jesus took our punishment for the bad things we do. He will not understand death very well, however.

Your child can learn that the Bible is God's Book and that it teaches us how to obey Him. It also teaches us all we know about God and Jesus. He can understand and enjoy stories from the Bible if they are told on his level. Get your child into the Bible. Bible storybooks are a good start. Show him a picture and build the story (on his level) around it, using your own words.

Pray with your child. Encourage him to pray. Have two kinds

of prayertimes—established times, such as at bedtime, and spontaneous times. Teach your child that praying is a natural and enjoyable way to talk to God. Prayer pleases God because He wants us to talk to Him. There will be times when your child is tired and cranky and may not want to pray with you. It is better not to force him to knuckle under but to be an example and to pray yourself. Remember, your child is a great imitator.

● *Ages 4-5.* Your child at four and five can think of God in a personal way. She understands that God is perfect and the Creator. She senses God's greatness and wonder. She can associate God with things that are good, true, and beautiful. It cannot be emphasized enough, however, that much of your child's concept of God the Father is related to her relationship with you. Can she trust you? Can she depend on your love and discipline? Do you show love to her in spite of her shortcomings? If you can say yes to these questions, then you have profoundly helped your child develop a better sense of who God is.

Your child can deal with Jesus as a personal friend. She can understand that Jesus is God's Son, but she will not understand the concept of the Trinity.

At this age, she is gaining a deeper understanding of the difference between right and wrong. Her conscience is emerging. She can know her wrong actions are sin in God's eyes. She can feel sorry for her sin and confess it. If you have expressed genuine forgiveness of her wrongdoings, she can better experience God's forgiveness. She needs to understand that God loves her even when she is bad.

Your child at age four or five can become a Christian in the true sense of the word, but let her grow into this in her own time. Too many parents have pushed their children into a decision for Christ when the children were neither ready intellectually nor spiritually. A child will often come to the Lord gradually without being able to identify a specific moment of decision.

The Bible can and should become an interesting and important book for your child. *The Living Bible* is easy to read, and your son or daughter will be able to understand much of the narrative. A picture Bible storybook is also excellent. Cultivate a time each day for Bible reading with your child. This will do much toward developing her love for the Word.

Your child can worship in a very real sense. She is naturally fascinated by new things she discovers each day. When her fascination and wonder are directed toward an appreciation of God and His greatness, worship becomes very natural and real for her. She may not understand God's invisibility, but she believes she can talk to Him. Singing and praising God is natural for your child. She loves rhythms and action songs. Sing along with her—she'll be delighted.

● *Ages 6-7.* Make God a constant subject of your conversation with your six- or seven-year-old. God is a real person who is part of your family life. Your child will probably ask where God is and why He cannot be seen. His understanding of God will remain somewhat vague in spite of your explanations. But he can understand some basic truths about God.

He can understand that God loves him, his family, his friends, and all the other people in the world as well. He can know and appreciate God's forgiveness for wrongs he has committed. He can understand that God's omnipotent power can make a person well or calm a storm. Bible stories that show God's power are exciting to him.

Your child can have a personal relationship with Jesus. He knows that he has committed sin (though the concept of a sinful nature is too abstract for him) and that this is not pleasing to God. He can understand and believe that God forgives him because Jesus accepted the punishment for his sin on the cross. He can also invite Jesus into his life and know that he belongs to God's family. He can look forward to living forever with God.

Do not pressure your child into a formal conversion experience. Let him initiate the decision himself. Concern yourself with providing him with sound Christian teaching that will prepare him to respond to God's call. Let him share in your relationship to Christ by encouraging him to pray, read the Bible, and obey God's commands. Pray for him daily, and let him know you are praying for him.

You can play a vital role in your child's relationship to Jesus. Have a time of personal devotions with him each day. Talk to Jesus with him. Talk about some Scripture with him, and relate the Word to specific situations in his life. He should have a children's Bible of his own.

Remember that biblical truth is best communicated relationally. This means that your example and the loving relationship you build with your child will convey more scriptural truth to him than long, lecture-type family devotions. Concentrate more on helping him understand concepts (such as what it means to love our enemies, what is meant by God's omnipotence) than on having him learn and memorize facts about the Bible (such as how many chapters there are in Acts).

● *Ages 8-11.* Your child should be able to recognize sin as sin when she hears stories of people doing wrong, but to identify her own sins is not so easy. However, she will naturally have a keen sense of justice. This will help her feel more responsible for her own wrongdoings. She now begins to understand why God must punish sin, that Jesus took the punishment, and that she needs to give her life to the Lord.

Because your child can now read, she will take new interest in the Bible if you encourage her to do so. Be sure she has a Bible of her own. A recent version with pictures and maps is best. When she is around ten years old, she can begin a habit of daily personal Bible reading. She will learn to do this much more readily if she knows you do it yourself.

Your child also loves to be read to. She particularly loves Bible stories that have plenty of action and heroes. However, she may be bored by stories she has heard many times. She will enjoy acting out Bible stories as well as listening to them.

She is now old enough to know in a deeper sense that the Bible is God's Word, that it is without error, that it is to be obeyed, and that it provides direct answers for many problems she faces in life. But she needs to be guided in finding those answers. She can memorize Scripture easily, but her memorization should be accompanied by explanations from you of the meaning of the Word's truths as they relate to her experiences.

Your child's sense of loyalty can be directed toward the church and the Lord. Jesus can also be a hero figure in your child's eyes. A personal relationship with Jesus is generally easy for an eight- to eleven-year-old. She can learn that she needs Jesus Christ to control her life. She can know that Jesus will help her with her fears. But how much of this she learns will depend to a great extent on your example.

● *Ages 12-14.* Because your junior-high child can grasp abstract concepts, he now can learn deep spiritual truths. He can begin to grasp the concept of the Trinity. He can have a much deeper understanding than ever before of what salvation means. The concepts of redemption, the sinful nature, and how Jesus bore our sins on the cross are all much clearer to him now. It would be wise to discuss these subjects with your child to see how much he understands. You can help him a great deal by clarifying certain things about which he may be confused.

Your child can have a much better understanding of what the body of Christ is all about. He can know what spiritual gifts are, though he may have difficulty identifying his own. If he has committed himself to Christ, he should be able to become a member of your church. He can understand the meaning of Communion, and after instruction he should be allowed to partake. His participation in church depends a great deal on your own involvement. If you are involved, he will be also; if not, he probably won't be either.

Your child will probably want to be involved in church. If he is a member, he will want to think he is a vital part of the body. He has the capacity to serve others. He wants and needs guided opportunities in leadership. Remember that your child is one of the church's future leaders. Active participation in a well-planned youth program will help develop his leadership skills.

Your child is now developing Christian values of his own. He is seeking answers to many questions he has about morals, ethics, and spirituality. He is beginning to question your values, and he may openly reject some of them. Deep inside he wants to do what is right and submit to God's authority, but he is searching for answers he can call his own. He will particularly question absolute guidelines imposed by his parents and church. He is very perceptive and quickly identifies hypocrisy and double standards.

This questioning and searching period is difficult for many Christian parents to face. You may see your child swaying in his faith. Feeling protective, you may argue with him and try to force on him what you believe is right. This may only drive him further away from you.

Your best approach is to encourage him to discuss his questions with you. Be open with him—express your feelings and beliefs, but allow him to disagree. Take the risk of treating him as an equal. Do not belittle him or think you must put him in his place. Realize that his searching and questioning approach is a healthy way to come to terms with spiritual matters on his own. In the end, he will be a much better Christian for it.

● *Ages 15-18.* Your teenager's experience and ability to do more sophisticated thinking enable her to think in deeper and more serious terms about spiritual things. She is still searching for her own answers about life and her relationship to God. She may develop a special interest in some rather complicated theological issues. If this happens, you can help her a great deal by encouraging her spiritual interests. Discuss her questions with her. Give her your insights and opinions, but avoid arguing. You can challenge her thoughts, but show respect for her opinions too.

If your child has been involved in church up to this point, she

SELF-ESTEEM IS VITAL IN MORALS AND FAITH

Healthy self-esteem is the foundation of moral and spiritual development. Without self-esteem, a child will not be secure in his moral choices and won't be able to make moral choices that consider the needs of others. Without healthy self-esteem, a child will be hindered in responding to God's love. If a child has not grown up with the experience of being unconditionally loved and a meaningful part of a family, he will have difficulty making the transition from faith in people to faith in the loving God.

The child's most basic image of God is the image created by the parents through their behavior in their relationship to the child. If this is negative, the child transfers that negative image onto his picture of God. If it is positive, the child will have a positive image of God.

So one of the most important tasks of parents is to build a basis of love and security on which the child can develop morality and faith.

Ronald Nikkel

may have a growing interest in being a vital part of the church. She thinks she is grown up and appreciates being treated that way. She is willing to take on more responsibility, and, if encouraged, she will appreciate opportunities to serve and lead. A wise church will do all it can to present older teens with such meaningful challenges.

Many fine opportunities for Christian service are also available to older teens through service-oriented organizations like Teen Missions. Other missionary organizations and camps offer short-term service opportunities. You will do well to encourage your child to get involved in such programs.

Obviously, not all children are interested in church activities. In her search for herself, your child may rebel against her parents and the church she grew up in. If your child has rejected you or the church, it is important that you seek to maintain an understanding relationship with her. This is vital.

Beyond seeking the Lord in prayer and depending on the Holy Spirit to work in your child's life, you can do little else. You do not necessarily need to blame yourself for her rejection. Your child is responsible for her own relationship to God. If you have provided her with a relatively secure family life, she may very well come back into the fold.

Making Your Faith Relevant to the Lives of Children
BRUCE & MITZIE BARTON

EXPERTS SAY THAT 80 PERCENT OF ALL ADULTS IN THE church have never read through the Bible completely. Few people read it regularly. Even fewer apply its lessons to everyday life. Most parents are very busy; they don't have time to be expert Bible scholars or theologians. Many parents don't even have time to stop and think. But in order to make Christianity relevant to the daily life and struggles of your child, you must read, understand, and act on timeless Bible truth.

Read. As a parent, you need a regular reading program in the Bible for the support, comfort, correction, and teachings that

God gives to help you in your daily life.

Understand. In order to understand the Bible more fully, you must think about the connection between the original setting and your own life situations. The more you are able to apply the Bible to all areas of your life, the more you are able to help your children see the relevance for their lives.

Act. It is not enough to read and understand the Bible; you must follow through by making your daily decisions and responses living examples of biblical principles.

Family devotions provide an opportunity to *read* portions of Scripture, to develop *understanding* through discussion, and to suggest how everyone can *act* to live out biblical principles. Family devotions enable parents to explain biblical events and to make applications to events or crises in the family's life. They enable the family to discuss real issues that emerge from reading the Bible story. When, for example, discussing Jesus' reaction to the lepers, it gave us an opportunity to discuss how to treat "unlovely" classmates.

As you relate Bible stories to present situations, Scripture can really come alive. If you are studying the life of David, you can talk about how he handled the hostility of King Saul and relate it to handling criticism from friends. If you are studying the healing of the paralyzed man in Mark 2, you can point out how his four friends brought him to see Jesus and discuss how to be a friend to someone who is in need.

During prayer time, ask your children to pray with you about financial concerns your family may be facing, or pray for personal struggles that relatives may have.

Holidays can be used as a way to bring home biblical concepts. We always use the four Sundays of Advent as a time of singing, praying, and sharing ideas related to the coming of Christ. We read Christmas stories not just from the Bible but also from other types of literature that honor Christ's birth. We also try to observe other holidays from the church calendar; for example, our family celebrates the Passover dinner with other families in order to teach Old Testament history and the meaning of Christ's sacrifice for us.

Anytime can be a time to share with our children. All the crises of life become ways for us to talk about faith. It is very difficult for sheltered kids to learn deep spiritual truth. Faith comes not only by hearing the Word of God and by loving relationships, but from testing. We need to be careful that we do not shield our children from trouble but share with them how to behave when troubles come. For instance, when a neighbor's house burned, we as a family prayed for them, gave them clothes and supplies, and discussed how temporary possessions are.

With preschoolers we can use nature, the stars in the sky, cycles of the weather, and animals in the zoo to talk about God as Creator and the love He showed when He made earth, animals, and people. We can show our children how God forgives by making sure that we clearly forgive them and ask forgiveness when we have done wrong. We can use bedtime prayers as a way to teach the protection and care that God provides. By reviewing each day, we can thank God for His kindness in the good things that happened that day and for His help with our problems.

School age provides the time for answering the ultimate questions of life. Many children wonder if their parents will ever get divorced. We need to share our commitment and love for our spouse and also our belief that God gives us the power and the discipline to make our marriage work. Quite often death—in the family or otherwise—provides an opportunity to discuss heaven and God's plan for man. When a friend's baby died, we showed how friends and relatives prayed for and helped them. We pointed out how the pastor visited every day. We explained how God uses people to do His work. Through this period, we need to help children grow beyond a magical, idealistic, romantic view of God and help them to see that He is the kind of God who works in us, through us, and in the community of believers.

Our children have missionary children as pen pals. As children from overseas share their living conditions, needs, and observations, it has been an eye-opening challenge to our family.

TV shows, cartoons, books, and movies provide a chance to talk about Christian values. Discuss what's good as well as what's bad.

Preteens deal with gossip, peer pressure, and criticism from friends at school. By showing how Christ helps us deal with the same issues, we show the relevance of Christianity. When children this age demonstrate tremendous character, reward them heartily. Our daughter baby-sat at a very messy house, and she cleaned up the place. When we heard about it, we complimented her for going beyond what was expected and for not being upset that she was not rewarded financially. When a family friend became divorced, we reviewed the meaning of Christian marriage.

In general, we try to point out connections between Bible truth and daily living. We talk to our kids about *our problems* and how Christ helps us. We also talk about problems *others face* and ask our children, "How should people handle such a situation?" We also urge our kids to talk about *their problems* and concerns and then show them how practical Christianity can be.

Out of the Church, into the World
DAVID & KAREN MAINS

THE CHRISTIAN ELEMENT OF OUR SOCIETY HAS BECOME A self-contained unit to the degree that it has its own publishing houses, its own stars, its own personalities. When Christians become a part of the church scene, their whole world begins to revolve around it. And then they begin evaluating life on the basis of whether or not they are enjoying that subculture.

That's just the opposite of what God wants us to do. He wants Christians to be the salt in society. And though we will never change society, we can contribute to it, preserve it, and provide for it things that are pleasing to God.

One way we've helped keep our kids from developing a Christian subculture mentality is to refrain from talking about witnessing. They do share their faith, but that's because we say such things as, "How can we show love to that person? He's really hurting." Or, "Can you think of ways we can minister to them?"

This type of thinking showed when Melissa decided to go to a public high school her senior year instead of finishing at the Christian school she had been attending. It was a hard decision, and we weren't sure it was the right choice. But when she got to the public school, Melissa related beautifully.

She was a good listener, and everyone started talking with her—girls who had had babies and then came back to school, girls who were then pregnant, the popular kids, kids with all the brains. Many of them commented on the fact that they'd never had a friend like Melissa.

Because that comment came up frequently, we sat down and talked about it. We discovered that Melissa demonstrated a care for different people, and one of the ways she showed it was to listen to what people had to say. Melissa didn't have to win the whole school to Christ. Her only goal was to show His love in whatever way she was able to do so.

Because we don't prod our kids to witness, the children relate beautifully in non-Christian environments. When Randall dates non-Christians, the conversations continually come around to Christian topics. Randy feels comfortable about his faith and has no trouble talking about it.

Their ease is quite different from what we experienced when we were growing up. At that time, people imposed on us how and in what ways we were to share our faith. This made talking about God very uncomfortable.

However, our kids are very comfortable with their faith. They know they are Christians. They know that to be a Christian isn't just something theological but that Christ lives in them and He teaches them how to love God and other people. They are very good at loving other people. They can pick out lonely kids or ones whose feelings have been hurt. Then they reach out to those kids.

We've shown our kids that not all that is good or interesting is in the church. We point out fascinating books; we take them to Shakespearean plays. We've said that there are lots of things in the world around us that a Christian can learn from and legitimately enjoy.

We've also exposed them to the suffering world. When we were in the inner city, we didn't have very much money. But when there were opportunities for the children to travel to developing Third World nations, we'd scramble to get the money together so that, even as young as junior high age, they could go. That helped them see that most of the world does not live in a middle-class environment.

If parents want to begin to wean their teens from the Christian subculture mentality, parents have to be willing to explore. They have to reach out to people who aren't like them. They might invite a family of a different race over for dinner or spend Thanksgiving at the Salvation Army or a mission. Or they may want to talk as a family about some of the people around them—people who are going through divorces or who have had crummy childhoods—and discover how they can understand and help these people.

You also need to talk about people as people, not just as Christians or non-Christians. For instance, a teacher can be a good or bad teacher whether he is a Christian or not.

We've also tried to maintain a relationship with the church that did not demand all of our kids' energy. That was one of the basic things David attempted when he started Circle Church. We tried to show that the church should equip you to be in the world and not consume all of your time. Thus, we only had Sunday morning services. Sunday evenings were for small neighborhood groups or for special projects. The whole thrust was to free the Christian family or the Christian single who was attending the church to have an outreach.

We've had a lot of different people in our home and have allowed each member of our family to ask those people questions. Not questions like, "What's your favorite color?" but ones like, "If you could be anybody else in the whole world besides yourself, who would you be?" or, "What are you learning spiritually?" They tend to ask questions that unlock the people. And these have been integration times, times when people of different ages and backgrounds can find out what each other is like.

We've worked at letting our kids fit into the church where they feel comfortable. Most churches divide people by age-groups, but that doesn't always meet people's needs. When Joel entered high school, he decided that he didn't want to be part of the small church youth group, but would rather sit in on the adult discussion groups. That was fine with us.

The kids' choices extend to the kinds of schools they attend. When we moved to Wheaton, we put our children in Christian schools. But after a few years, they were crawling the walls. (There's nothing wrong with the Christian schools; they were just too confining for our children.) The kids wanted to be out where they could test their faith, be challenged, and where they could see evidence of the blood of Christ at work in them.

Because the older kids both had good experiences, we put

Joel into public school when he started high school. It's incredible to see the way he integrates his faith.

One way he does it is with contemporary music. He uses it as a fantastic entry point for spiritual discussions. Once he tried to do this by working on the dance committee. His goal was to be able to use some contemporary Christian music at the dance.

It didn't work. But a funny thing happened. One day our pastor asked for prayer requests, so Joel asked him to pray that they could have contemporary Christian music at the school dance. We were "dying" (to use contemporary lingo), but it didn't phase Joel because that's how he was attempting to integrate his faith.

We try to let our kids make their own decisions as to how they move in and out of the Christian subculture. Of course, if we see areas that are potentially dangerous, we point them out. But if the children feel they want to go ahead, we usually allow them to do so.

That takes us back to Joel and the dance committee. We had tremendous reservations about his plan because we thought that using Christian music at a dance was a clash of cultures, not an integration of cultures. Anyhow, it didn't work out because the school decided to hire a live band to perform at the dance.

But the Lord honored Joel's desire just the same. One of his teachers asked Joel to do his juggling routine in his class on the last day of school. Since Joel had put a track of Christian records together for the dance, he was able to use that music as the background for his juggling routine. And teachers from other classes who came and watched invited Joel to do his routine in their classes as well.

The intent of Joel's heart was to share something that meant a great deal to him, to communicate his faith in Christ. The Lord knew that and gave him an opportunity to do it.

Helping Teens Apply Their Faith
WARREN WIERSBE

HELPING TEENS APPLY THEIR FAITH TO EVERYDAY LIFE IS A balance of teaching and modeling. It's an outgrowth of your own walk with God, and it needs to begin long before children reach their teens.

In our home, my wife and I had daily devotions individually, and we also had family devotions so the kids could see how it was done.

Less overtly but perhaps more importantly, we tried to show how the Word of God applied in daily life and how we should obey regardless of the circumstances. We didn't always succeed—sometimes we lost our patience—but we tried to see every experience as an opportunity to learn from the Lord and teach our children.

For example, whenever we've made a move, we've included the children in the praying and planning. Another instance was when I was hospitalized after a car accident. My wife is the hero here—she did a wonderful job comforting the children when it was uncertain whether I would live or die. With calm and poise, she took care of details and let the children know that God was in control.

In these and other situations, we tried to instill two principles:

First, *faith is not feeling, nor is it intellectual assent.* Faith is obeying God in spite of feelings, circumstances, or consequences. There's too much fuzzy "faith in faith" around today—the kind of stuff you hear about in the song, "I believe for every drop of rain that falls a flower grows." Nonsense. If that were true, we'd be up to our armpits in flowers.

Or there's a commercial faith—"God, I'll believe *if* You do this for me." That's not faith at all, and we've tried to steer clear of that.

We've tried to teach our kids the kind of faith the three young Hebrew men had in Daniel 3—"The God we serve is able to save us . . . but even if He does not . . . we will not serve your gods or worship the image of gold you have set up" (vv. 17-18, NIV). That faith means obeying God no matter what.

Second, *we don't live by explanations but by promises.* Everyone loves to speculate why God does this and why God allows that. When those questions come up, I've consistently told my kids, "I don't know." But I try to point them to a promise in Scripture.

Explanations may actually produce opposite results than intended. Some of the toughest faith problems happen in Bible

HOW GOD SOLVES OUR PROBLEMS

We need to teach teens how God solves problems. It's not usually by providing a convenient miracle. No, instead, this is the way He normally works.

He gives us:

- The courage to face our problems honestly.
- The wisdom to understand what's happening.
- The strength to do what we must.
- The faith to trust Him to do what we cannot.

This is how we taught our children that God solves problems. Where does the Word of God come in? It's woven into each step.

- Through the promises of the Word, we get the courage to face problems without running away or blaming someone else.
- Through the principles of the Word, we get the wisdom to understand, perhaps not everything we'd like to know, but the insight we need.
- Through the power of the Word, we get the strength to do what we must.
- Through persistence in the Word, we grow in faith.

We tried to teach our kids not to use the Bible as a crisis tool. If you're in the Word day after day and a crisis comes, you don't need to panic. You'll be ready for it.

Warren Wiersbe

colleges and seminaries where the Bible becomes a textbook, and Scripture loses its aura and mystery.

Faith is a relationship to God, not a complete understanding. I can have a great relationship with my surgeon and not know a scalpel from a screwdriver. There's a temptation these days, with all the study Bibles and Christian books, to live on explanations. You can't! The deeper you get in the Christian life, the less you can explain. I can't explain prayer—I really can't. But I pray now more than ever.

So we've tried to raise our children on promises rather than attempts to explain God's actions.

How do you make Scripture alive for teens, or for anyone? Martin Luther said it comes through study, prayer, and suffering. He pointed to Psalm 119, where over and over again the writer experiences those very things. Every third or fourth verse mentions some trial he's going through.

Families that want their teens to grow in faith can expect trouble. Don't run from it. Use it. Faith that can't be tested can't be trusted. Going through the furnace is the challenge and the opportunity.

But the key is using your own walk with God to demonstrate what the Christian life is. I really don't know any other way to do it.

What Teens Should Know about the Bible
WARREN WIERSBE

MANY TEENAGERS HAVE A NEGATIVE ATTITUDE TOWARD the Bible. One reason is that they see it as an oppressive rule book. That's largely because they haven't been taught that rules are merely one level of growing in the Word of God.

There are many levels of Bible content. We begin with stories that teach *lessons*. Little children should learn, for instance, that Moses lost his temper and he suffered for it. And this leads to *rules*. We shouldn't lose our temper. We shouldn't lie. And so on.

But rules embody *principles* that help us decide how to live in the complex situations we face. And these principles exist because God has a certain kind of *character*.

And the character of God leads us to His *promises*. This is a step that many people miss. Promises involve certain conditions, and meeting those conditions builds our character.

So teens need to see that the Bible is more than rules. It's a book full of principles and promises too, which help us mature and develop character.

A second reason for teens' negative attitudes toward the Bible is that they think it's irrelevant. Cain killed Abel. Peter lied about Jesus. So what? Besides pointing out character and principles, we must show them that the Bible—though completely factual—is a book of metaphor and symbols, which also fill teenage music. (That's one reason adults often can't understand it.)

From the very beginning of Scripture, we hit metaphor—light and darkness. The Bible pictures the Word as food, as a sword to defend us, as water to cleanse us. When teens begin to see the Bible not merely as a storybook but as food for the soul—that truth is to the spirit what food is for the body—then they begin to appreciate Scripture and learn from it.

These are the broad strokes necessary for teens. A few specifics should also be mentioned. First, they should know how the Bible is put together; it's fundamental to learn the books of the Bible.

Second, they should begin memorizing portions of Scripture. During our children's formative years, we were fortunate to be in a church with a marvelous Sunday School that emphasized memorization, and they got a lot of excellent foundational material.

Finally, they should see their parents (as well as the church) using the Bible creatively: not just as any other book to read. Nor as a magical, mystical book of incantations to ward off bad things. But a genuine, creative approach where the Word of God enters our lives, changes us, and God through us changes our circumstances.

Resources That Help Teenagers Grow Spiritually
JAMES GALVIN

CHURCH LIBRARIES, PUBLIC LIBRARIES, AND CHRISTIAN bookstores contain many resources to help teenagers grow spiritually. Often these resources are overlooked by parents or set aside because they don't know how to plug their teenagers into them. Some teenagers appear disinterested in reading books that would help their spiritual growth, and others seem to be disinterested in reading altogether. Parents who have tried to get their teenagers to read often feel that they can lead teenagers to the library, but they cannot make them read. So how can these resources best be used? How can parents interest teenagers in reading to help them grow spiritually?

One approach is to take a monthly trip to the church library or public library to explore the selection of books which may be of interest to the teenager. Church libraries often make the newest and most interesting books for young people a top priority. Though this is the least expensive approach, some teenagers are just bored by libraries. A second approach is to purchase a book for a teenager and wrap it up as a gift. Rather than waiting for a birthday, giving this type of gift, for no other reason except love and the desire to see him grow spiritually, will be a surprise and may help him read that particular book. Of course, some teenagers may start to read the book and never finish. Given this situation, a third approach might be to set up a reading program

TYPES OF RESOURCES	HELPS TEENAGERS GROW SPIRITUALLY THROUGH:
1. *Bible study.* Books about a particular section of the Bible or reference works, such as commentaries or Bible dictionaries. These examine the Scriptures in detail and also discuss the original language, history, culture, and archaeology.	Answering more in-depth, advanced questions about the Bible and theology; providing richer insights for living out their faith.
2. *Self-help.* Books dealing with a particular topic such as dating loneliness, etc. or those by famous authors which are more general in nature.	Offering practical help with a problem area in life or additional information in an area of interest.
3. *Biographies.* Life stories of Christians who have faced particular struggles in life.	Inspiring them to follow the examples of other Christians; providing role models to pattern their lives after.

4. *Fiction.* Creative writing which takes the form of mysteries, poems, short stories, or novels.	Viewing human struggles and spiritual struggles in life from a fresh perspective.
5. *Devotional aids.* Supplemental material for daily personal devotions.	Challenging them to apply Christian principles to everyday situations.
6. *Discipleship manuals.* Workbooks for spiritual growth specifically geared for teenagers to study in small groups.	Establishing basic disciplines of prayer, Bible study, and church involvement, and examining their actions from a biblical perspective.
7. *Magazines.* General Christian magazines or those targeted specifically for teenagers such as *Campus Life.*	Presenting Christian truth through attention-grabbing, easy-to-read magazine format.
8. *Audio cassettes.* Tapes on a particular topic or from a speaker of interest to teenagers.	Listening to a dynamic communicator when convenient.
9. *Christian music.* Music with lyrics relating to spiritual growth or Christian living.	Expressing feelings and solidifying convictions about their commitment to Jesus Christ.

where parents can take their teenager to a Christian bookstore to purchase any book of his choice. The only ground rules are the teenager must read the entire book that he selects and he may not select another book until the first book is completed. This approach will ensure the teenager is interested in the book, but he might not choose a book that the parents consider valuable for helping him grow spiritually.

Resources for spiritual growth, normally found in a Christian bookstore, would tend to fall into nine categories. The chart on the following page describes each and explains how it may be useful for helping teenagers grow spiritually.

For teenagers who like to read or are at least willing to do the hard work of reading to dig out some valued information, a book can be a very helpful resource. Many books are available that are written specifically for teenagers. Best-selling books, however, should not be overlooked. These are often self-help books with practical advice for a problem a teenager may be facing. Bible study books that are more detailed and academic in nature should also be considered for those who are bored by Sunday School classes or typical devotional materials. A more in-depth and adult approach may be exactly what they need to help them grow spiritually.

For teenagers who dislike reading, other resources such as magazines, music, and cassette tapes can facilitate spiritual growth. The text in these materials is often broken into short paragraphs with plenty of pictures, illustrations, and titles. Teenagers who might not ordinarily sit down to read a book would find it easier to use these resources. Even those who are poor readers can still grow spiritually through cassette tapes and Christian music.

In order to multiply the effectiveness of these resources, have teenagers study a book or listen to a tape together with a group of friends. This can be accomplished as a project in the youth group, or an assignment for a Sunday School class, or a special small group with an adult leader. Because of the influence of peers at this age, a group of teens reading through a biography, working through a discipleship manual, or reading through a best-selling book will do even more for helping teens grow spiritually.

CHAPTER
10

How Do I Help
My Child Get More
Out of Church?

My Kids Don't Like Church
RONALD HUTCHCRAFT

SOCIETY HAS CHANGED. ONLY A FEW YEARS AGO YOU were the odd one if your car didn't leave the driveway on Sunday morning to go to church. Now you're the odd one if it does. The family is weaker; the neighbors don't go, and probably church is the ultimate example of that old saying, "You can lead a horse to water, but you can't make him drink." You can get your kid to church, but that doesn't mean he's going to get anything out of it.

You can do everything possible to navigate your child's body through the church doors, and his mind can still stay home. Just getting his body to occupy a pew is not the point—occupying his heart with the Christian message and Christian fellowship is.

● *Why kids turn off.* Let's talk about some of the reasons why kids turn off *at* church—or *to* the church. One reason is *inconsistency.* They are quick to see the gap between what a leader is *teaching* and how he is *living.* They may even see the inconsistency between what that leader is teaching and how his own children, who might be their friends, are acting.

Another reason is *irrelevance*. Teens feel, perhaps, that there is no connection between what's going to happen to them on Monday morning and what is being taught on Sunday morning. And when they don't see a connection, they say, "What's the use of being here?"

A third reason is *independence*. They seem to say, "Anytime you want to make me do something, I want to show that I don't have to do it." And the more we try to force kids to go to church, the more their adolescent, independent feelings rebel against that. They have something to prove now, something to win. It's a power struggle.

A fourth reason some teens turn off *at* or *to* church is that there may be *a lack of others their age*. The most important factors to any teenager about any event are, "How many kids will be there?" and "Which kids?" And if he sees only a few kids his own age, that may just confirm his feelings that what's going on there is irrelevant.

A final reason is *school pressure*. Quite frankly, kids are in an academic and social pressure cooker at school. And if they're trying to make it in these areas, they may say that they don't have much time to spend at church. They have a time-management problem. They may really want to go to church but don't think they have time.

● *Freedom within boundaries.* Probably the best way to create a more positive attitude is to give teens latitude within limits; to give them freedom within boundaries. In other words, there are some things about their church relationship that *you* will decide. They won't get a choice. But *within* that structure they will have choices. For example, they will be allowed to choose with whom they will sit. Within the boundary that they must go to church, give them some freedom to choose which services they want to attend. Perhaps the policy decision will be two services a week. If that is the decision, you may allow them to decide *which* two services. You may even decide to allow them the freedom to choose *which* church to attend. Sometimes parental ego comes into play here because we want our kids to go to *our* church and be seen by *our* friends. But if they find a church that better ministers to their needs, there are cases

143

where we ought to allow them to choose another church fellowship. The point is to give your kids freedom to choose within your broader guidelines.

Now, what can parents tell kids to help them appreciate church and get more out of it?

● *Help kids appreciate church.* Help them realize that everyone at church is a becomer, including them. Nobody has "arrived"; everyone is "under construction," spiritually. No church is perfect. Fortunately, it's a place for imperfect people, or else you and I wouldn't be admitted. Yes, churches are made up of imperfect people, but people who are basically trying to grow up spiritually.

Encourage your kids to go to church to hear from God, not from people. Tell them, "You never know what you'll hear from Him. It isn't just the sermon; maybe it will be in a hymn, maybe in what the choir sings, maybe in the pastoral prayer, maybe in something that someone says before or after the service. But the point is: Go into the service saying, 'God, I'm here to hear Your message. I don't know which person You're going to send it through.' That means you've got to be looking everywhere because you never know where God will make that personal encounter with you."

Put yourself into it, and you'll get more out of it. If you're not getting anything out of it, you may not be putting anything into it. Start to take some notes; really listen; make an effort to make an application. Kids are used to spoon-feeding these days. They're used to TV and other media just handing it to them, and it takes a little work and extra energy to get something out of church.

Sit in an active rather than a passive spot. The church is one of the only places I know where people get there early to get a back seat; everywhere else you go, you get there early to get a front seat. You're saying by the position of your body, "I want to be out of here." I challenge kids for just one month to try sitting on the first three rows, taking notes, and really being active, front-end sinners. The closer you sit, the better it is. Don't sit in an active spot and be passively out of it.

Go to church determined to get a personal word from the Lord. Say, "God, I'm not leaving here without more of You. Somewhere here today I'm going to get more of You."

Go to church to *give* something, not just to get something. We tend to see the pastor and the choir as the performers, and we in the congregation as the audience when, in fact, the biblical concept of worship is that the pastor, the musicians, and the congregation are all the performers, and God is the audience. What we're doing in church is for Him. So the question might be, "Did God get anything out of this service from me?"

Look for a place to serve. Fans at football games spend a lot of their time criticizing what the players are doing. The players spend *their* time playing the game. If kids come to church with a fan mentality, they're going to sit and think about all the ways things could be done differently. My challenge is: Get in the game. Find a place to serve. Don't sit on the sidelines and criticize.

If you go to church determined that someone is there who needs a smile, a touch, a listening ear, an encouraging word from you, you'll be a blessing and a true servant of Christ. This way church can never be a failure for you.

Finally, prepare for worship before you go, whether that means reviewing memory verses on Saturday night for Sunday School, reading a passage you know the pastor will be tackling the next morning, or singing together or praying on the way to church. Create that air of expectation before you get there.

● *How families can help.* Here are some practical things families can do to help enrich the church experience for kids:

First, discuss applications. For instance, "Let's each talk about what we got from the Lord this morning and what we are going to do this week because of something we heard in church today." If that becomes a regular fixture in the family agenda, you'll all tend to be looking for something to talk about. *Tie the lessons of Sunday into your daily family devotions during the week.*

Second, minimize the Sunday morning hassle. We've all been guilty of bickering all morning long, then suddenly putting on a smile as we walk through the church doors. But, of course, that behavior doesn't exactly create a climate in which the Lord can speak to us. Why not plan ahead? Get the clothes ready Saturday night. Set the alarm a little earlier. Eliminate the things that tend to make Sunday morning a negative time; try to make it peaceful and positive so that the family goes to the house of the Lord with that attitude.

Third, invite church families to your home who match your family. This will help create a sense of socialness as well as spiritualness about what goes on at church.

Fourth, do all you can to encourage your kids with church friendships. Invite those kids over; have parties at your house for them.

By doing the things I've mentioned, you're saying to your kids, "Listen, for the next three months, six months, or whatever, I want to see you give our church your best shot. After that, if you've really given it your best shot, and your spiritual needs are still unmet, we are willing to let you start to search for another church." That's the way kids should earn the right to make their own choices about church.

SURVIVING SUNDAY SKIRMISHES

"As long as you're living under this roof, you will go to our church!"

"What do you mean you don't feel like going? What kind of Christian are you anyway?"

"I don't care where your friend goes to church; you're coming with us!"

Sound familiar? In many Christian homes, teenagers resist going to their parents' church. Only after verbal warfare or outright coercion do they shuffle out and go along for the ride. Feelings range from silent apathy to open rebellion. Some parents simply give up and allow their children to attend another church or sleep in.

This can be painful for parents, especially when they are longtime church members. Church involvement represents years of commitment—tithing, teaching Sunday School, serving on boards and committees. They may have helped build the church and still have the zeal and vision that gave birth to their local assembly.

Other parents simply want to do what's right. They know a solid foundation in the Bible and church involvement are important in a young life.

Your teenagers are emerging adults and question every part of society, including its morals. They desire independence and the opportunity to make their own decisions. This is healthy, though it can be threatening to the older generation. Your child's Christianity needs to be deeper than a parroting of your views.

Be open to your teen's questions and criticisms, and learn from them. Encourage him to probe his faith at a deeper level and search Scripture for direction in church attendance. This present conflict can be an opportunity to discuss spiritual truths.

Take an honest look at your own church attendance. Why do you go to church? Do you attend church for social reasons or just out of habit? Admit when you're wrong and pray for a fresh touch of God's Spirit.

What kind of model are you? Is "roast minister" regular fare for Sunday dinner? Don't be surprised if your children pick up your critical attitudes. Though you can't undo years of teaching in a week or two, it's not too late to change. Speak in love and affirm the pastor, services, and programs.

What are your priorities? Is church really important to you? Does it make any difference in your life? Actions can be deafening. Some parents forbid their children to attend another church, but later allow them to miss their own church if they have to work on Sunday. Sometimes, the real reason parents require their teen to join them in church on Sunday is to save face. Are you embarrassed to explain your son's or daughter's absence? Your young people will see right through you.

Listen to your teen with sensitivity. His complaints may be symptoms of adolescence or echoes of your complaints from months ago. Then respond with loving acceptance and instruction.

"Provoke not your children to wrath: but bring them up in the nurture and admonition of the Lord" (Eph. 6:4, kjv).

David Veerman

Teenagers and Church:
Why the Two May Not Mix
HOWARD HENDRICKS

ONE REASON TEENS AND CHURCH MAY NOT MIX IS BE-
cause teens go unprepared. Most people have never been taught
how to get something out of church. They walk through the
church doors and expect something magical to happen to them.
Of course, too much "get" and too little "give" isn't right either.
We need to honestly ask if we go to church to delight God's
heart, or just to get our spiritual "goodies."

Another reason our teens may resist church is because we
don't debrief them afterward. In other words, do we discuss at
the table what went on at church? Do we ever ask, "What did
you think of the sermon?" "What are your questions?"

As parents we also have to ask ourselves if we build bridges
with the pastoral staff. Do we have them over to the house? Do
we support the church or do we criticize it?

Parents often criticize the youth leader and then wonder why
their teen doesn't want to be involved. Once there were two
couples slicing the throat of our youth director. Their kids were
giving us more grief than anyone else in the group because the
parents were undermining the director's position.

We finally called them before the board and asked them to tell
us all of their criticisms. We told them we would work with the
youth director on the problems, but that we didn't want them
criticizing the youth director in front of anyone. When the parents stopped criticizing the youth director, the teens became
more involved.

Should Parents Make Teens Go to Church?
Developing a positive attitude for going to church starts when
the children are small. If the parents go to church with a sense of
enthusiasm, the children will pick this up and model the positive
attitude.

But if a teen doesn't want to go to church, I would treat the
situation with a precision touch. I wouldn't *make* him go to

church but, on the other hand, I wouldn't *ignore* the problem. I would explore it at a deeper level.

DOES YOUR TEEN HAVE TO ATTEND YOUR CHURCH?

Two of the goals that Christian parents are trying to achieve with their children are family togetherness and individual spiritual development.

If a teenager doesn't want to attend your church, it can be for a variety of reasons. He's either trying to get away from you, or he finds something attractive in another church. Maybe he's avoiding some difficulty at your church.

It's important that you attempt to find the real reason. If he's trying to get away from you, then the issue is one of conflict resolution between you and the teenager. If he finds spiritual fulfillment or excitement at another church, then you must evaluate its spiritual health (doctrine, leadership, approach to issues, etc.), your reasons for staying where you are, and the time when the family can be together.

If there is a difficulty or problem that he is trying to avoid at your church, then you need to evaluate whether it is worth trying to solve. In this situation you can either try to change a legitimately negative situation, or you can teach your teenager what it means for him to provide positive leadership and not to run in the face of difficulties. Since there are different answers for different problems, we must follow the advice of Solomon and seek wisdom from a multitude of counselors (Prov. 11:14).

Larry Kreider

Not wanting to go to church is often a sign of independence. Somewhere along the line, the teen has to tell you no just to "try it on for size," to find out if he really is independent. If the parents have a good sense of humor and don't make a big issue out of it, they might nip this behavior in the bud. They might respond with something like, "Oh, come on, you're going along. We're all going as a family. You can't let us down." They sweep him up, and they have a lot of fun, and go out to eat afterward. By the next Sunday, he's probably forgotten about it.

If the teen has a serious gripe about going to church, parents could replace church attendance with another assignment. Options the teen could be given might include personal Bible study or getting involved with other people in ministry. By doing this, you get away from outward conformity and concentrate on inward conviction. Maybe the family needs to find a new church. Of course, in some communities there *are* no other churches, and the parents have to face that realistically.

The key is to keep the relationship open between you and the teen. If you have a knock-down-drag-out fight, and you lose the relationship, then whether the teen goes to church or not is really quite immaterial.

It's like the parents whose daughter comes home announcing she is going to marry a certain man, and the parents reply, "If you marry him, you'll never step in this house again." I've known young women who go out and marry the man, and when I ask them why, they say, "I hated the man, but my father said if I did it, I'd never come home again. I thought, *Well, I'll show him.*"

We need to guard against church attendance becoming a battle like that—where teens feel they must show us we don't have power over them.

What the Church Can Do to Get Kids Involved
B. CLAYTON BELL

A CHURCH HAS TO BE CAREFUL NOT TO EQUATE ITS ACTIvities with living the Christian life. The church's program should be a supplement and an encouragement to a person's relationship with the Lord. It should not be *equated* with one's relationship to God. Even a church's teaching ministry should be a supplement to Christian teaching in the home. Unfortunately, a lot of families don't realize this and rely entirely on the church for Christian training.

A church should provide wholesome activities for its youth, but these should simply supplement, not compete with, what the family does. The youth activities provided depend on the size and resources of the individual church. We have tried various things in the different sized churches my wife and I have served. These churches have run the gamut from 110 members where there was no other staff, not even a secretary, to the very large congregation we're in now.

In the smaller church, we had an open house for the young people where we sat down with them and discussed their needs. Occasionally, we took them places and once a year we went to a conference together. We didn't have any bang-up program going, but the kids knew that we were interested and concerned, so they responded. They felt like I was not just the adults' pastor but their pastor too, and that made a difference. We also planned cooperative youth programs with other churches in the community for cookouts, discussions, and other events.

In the very large church I pastor now, we have six people working just with young people, so we are able to provide a wide variety of activities. We have a gymnasium, take more than 100 kids each year to out-of-state conferences, have parties in homes, and schedule many events. We plan some of our youth activities just for sheer fun. Kids like to get together, so we often get two busloads of kids and take them to an out-of-town football game and stop for pizza on the way back. That way the kids get together; they are able to do something wholesome; there are just enough parents involved to make sure everything is on the up-and-up; and yet it's a large enough group to make the kids feel they are on their own.

A church should plan its youth programs and activities in conjunction with the parents. We've encouraged each of our youth ministers to counsel with parents and some of the young people on a regular basis, so that they can get periodic feedback from both groups on how the programs are going and what the needs and opportunities are.

It's a debatable point, however, as to how much responsibility teens should be given in the life of the church. Some people believe that church government needs to be shared by the youth. They strongly emphasize the importance of having young people serve on official boards. Other people believe that the official government of the church must be in the hands of the spiritually mature, though these leaders need to have their ears open to what the young people are saying.

HOW PARENTS CAN HELP THE CHURCH

The best thing parents can do to help the church do its job better is to raise a good kid. Then that kid will help other kids.

In every church, certain teens are the transformers, the Daniels and Josephs. They can have more spiritual influence than a legion of adults. So as a parent, my first responsibility is at home.

If, however, I find my teen being harmed by what happens at church, I must do something. Of course, I'll be more careful not to make hasty accusations because maybe, just maybe, it isn't the church's fault but mine— or my kid's.

But if the problem genuinely seems to lie with the church, I'd go to the youth leader—not the pastor. I'd say something like, "I've noticed our kids aren't spending much time with their Bibles," or "I've been quizzing my son and he isn't remembering anything from Sunday School. What can we do to help?" By offering your concern and assistance, you're much more likely to find the youth leader willing to make changes.

One other specific suggestion: get parents and youth workers together every couple of months for a "Christian PTA" meeting. We did that, and though it wasn't highly organized, it greatly aided parents in knowing what their teens were doing and how they could reinforce the lessons at home.

Warren Wiersbe

I think that young people should be supplied opportunities to give their input into what's going on in the church. As far as getting them to help serve, however, their attention spans are often too short to sit through long committee meetings. And you can't expect a young person to be as seriously interested in everything that goes on in the church as an adult is. To expect that is to frustrate him and disappoint the church.

A different type of problem occurs when a church leader's teenager doesn't want to attend the youth programs, which can be pretty embarrassing to the parent. You're asking for rebellion, however, if you tell teenagers they have to attend because of the leadership role you play in the church. And your embarrassment if they don't go is no strong motivation for them to respond in a different way. Besides, their responsibility is to the Lord. In such situations, I talked to my teenagers about being salt and light in a group and suggested that they go and try to make it a better group. Sometimes I pushed our kids a little to be involved but, every now and then, I also let them get out of participating.

RETREAT!

"Retreat" is a curious name for a weekend experience designed for spiritual and physical renewal and for personal challenge. In reaction, some have renamed these experiences "advances." Whatever the name, retreats, camps, and conferences provide excellent opportunities for reflection, fellowship, and renewed commitment.

If the budget and schedule permit, teenagers should be encouraged to get away and spend time "retreating" occasionally. (Of course, the trips should have reputable and responsible organizers and sponsors.) Often, however, our kids don't want to go or react with benign disinterest. This is especially true for younger teens (their first retreat). In these situations, it would be counterproductive to force them to go. Instead, we should find out why they are uninterested. Perhaps they are afraid to leave home; they don't think *they* can afford it; or they haven't been "sold" on the trip. Usually, however, the block involves their friends. It's threatening to go *alone* (adults have the same feelings).

Most of these obstacles can be overcome by careful and loving help. If money is the problem (and we really want them to go), we can offer to pay for part or *all* of it. If they just aren't convinced of its value or that they will have a good time, we can enlist the help of the youth leaders. They will be happy to encourage our son or daughter and to reassure him or her of their presence and friendship.

Working with other parents will help encourage *groups of friends* to make the trip. These parents may also want to chip in for a "scholarship fund" to help those who really can't afford the cost.

If there isn't a specific camp or retreat on the horizon, we can research camps together and find one that meets their needs. (A "sports" camp would be inappropriate if they aren't athletic.) To help them make the decision, we can offer incentives.

Before and after camp, we must respect their feelings, allowing them to honestly evaluate the experience. (If they didn't like it, we should drop it.)

Hopefully, they will have had a wonderful time retreating from the daily schedule, meeting new friends, having fun, and deepening their understanding of themselves, others, and God.

YFC Editors

This is where parents need to set the example for their children. If parents continually complain about the church, the minister, the music, etc., and go only sporadically themselves, the kids will quickly get the message that they don't have to go and that church is not important. No matter how poor the preacher is, I have found I can always worship the Lord in church. But if the church is so bad that you can't do even that, then you should look for another church.

If you as parents don't like what is happening in the youth program, then talk with the youth director and explain the problem that's bothering you. If necessary, sit down with the minister or with the church board and explain how you think things should be changed.

The greatest thing that parents can offer the church is to realize that the church is not an end in itself; it is a means to an end. The church is to help us grow in a relationship with the living Christ, to assist our learning about and worshiping Him, and to provide us this channel through which we can express our loyalty and worship. Parents need to communicate to teen-agers that their loyalty should be to the Lord, and the church is just the channel through which they serve Him.

The Sunday Search
DAVID & KAREN MAINS

AS PARENTS OF FOUR CHILDREN AGES THIRTEEN TO TWEN-ty-two, we have learned through the years that it is important to prepare for Sunday church worship. Preparation allows us to actively participate in what is going on and to discover what the Lord is teaching us through His Word. That is why we have invented a family game, the Sunday Search.

The first rule of the game is to approach a worship experience with the expectation that Christ will speak to us. We look for the answer to the question, "How will Christ speak *to me* today?"

Christ might speak to us many times and in many places: through the sermon, in Sunday School class, through particular Scripture passages or hymns, during a quiet period in the service, or in a conversation with someone before or after the service.

The attitude we encourage is this: "The Lord has a special message for me today, and I don't want to miss it." This mindset prepares every member of the family for the special encounters with Christ that will naturally occur to those who are vigilant and expectant.

The second rule is to discover how Christ will speak *through me.* We feel strongly that Christians do not go to church only to receive, but also to give to the Lord in worship and to contribute to the body of Christ, the community of believers. This is part of the dynamic of church life. The work of Christ operates both ways—to us and through us. We might find Christ speaking through us as we teach a class or encourage someone or even minister through touch.

I (David) remember one morning when I was really in trouble. I got a very nasty phone call before church, and I had a headache all morning after that. Our older son, Randy, was home from college that weekend, and he sat next to me in church.

About halfway through the sermon, he put his arm around me and grabbed my shoulder. He kept his hand there for ten minutes or so. I felt as though strength was coming from his hand, healing me. He was totally unaware that I had a problem, but through him my headache went away. I believe the Lord ministers to us that way, through other believers.

Sometimes Christ speaks through us when we are led to invite someone to church or when we lead a person to the Lord. It's thrilling to think that Christ actually uses us to communicate with others, and as we have searched for these experiences of Christ working through us on Sundays, we have seen amazing things happen.

The third rule is that when we get together as a family at dinner or some other time, we talk about these experiences of Christ speaking to us and through us. This has strengthened us as a family and has helped us understand how the various members of the body of Christ operate in concert. It has also made our children much more aware of the contributions they can make.

We never force any members of our family to participate, but that has never been a problem. They seem to delight in hearing what other people have to say, and one experience leads to another as we share around the table. It's a little like Tom Sawyer painting the fence—as we begin to talk with each other, the children *want* to join and participate. It's like handing out paintbrushes!

In our game we see some principles of small-group dynamics in action. Those who might not be the first to share eventually get drawn in, eager to tell what happened to them and how they experienced Christ.

Often children react positively to something that might not have reached the adults at all. A lot of what we see in church is old hat to us; it's hard to see it freshly. But our children may report what they heard as if it were totally new and the best idea they've heard all week. The Word is implanted in different hearts in different ways.

QUALITY TIME IN CHURCH

As parents, we are responsible to help set an attitude toward church that will affect our children for the rest of their lives. It is important that parents not set up barriers for their children by implying that church is boring or by showing indifference to what is going on there. Parents have a tremendous amount of influence here, and their own attitudes speak loudly. Enthusiasm and willing participation go a long way.

That doesn't mean that parents have to attend every church service and activity that's offered. It's not how many programs you and your family attend during the week that determines your spiritual life and growth. Rather, parents should know why they are in church in the first place, and then they should take what is offered by the church and make it meaningful in their own lives.

David & Karen Mains

We have shared this game with people in our radio audience of "Chapel of the Air," and it is now being used and tested in the lives of our listeners. The feedback we are getting is good. Though it is a simple idea, we believe it is a revolutionary tool. When people use it, they get serious about worship and participate in it more.

The interesting thing is that the church service may not have changed at all, but children's and adults' attitudes change once they see themselves as part of Christ's work in the world through the church. The game allows us to share the best with each other. It gives us all new appreciation of the many facets of Christ's work in the body.

"I'm Bored!"
MARLENE LeFEVER

"SUNDAY SCHOOL IS SO BORING!" IT'S A COMMON COM-
plaint, and parents are often at a loss to answer it. Actually, there
are a number of things parents can do when their children seem
uninterested in Sunday School:

1. *Get excited about church and Sunday School yourself.*
When parents ask me how to revive their children's interest in
Sunday School, I tell them that the best thing they can do is
begin to have a personal interest in Sunday School themselves.
We can't blame our children for not being excited about their
Sunday School class if we don't attend or get excited about our
own.

If parents start attending adult classes and talking favorably
about them, their example on Sunday mornings and in follow-up
during the week will speak louder than any admonition that
"Sunday School is good for you" (so, no doubt, is cabbage).

2. *Check out your child's class and classroom.* Visiting a
child's age-level class will help a parent discover firsthand what
goes on there each week. He or she will be able to observe the
quality of interaction between teacher and students and perhaps
find out if there are any reasons for the child's poor performance
or boredom.

Environmental conditions make a difference in how people
respond to learning. An atmosphere can be conducive to learning, or it can directly discourage it. The temperature, for example, can make the difference between alert children and passive,
sleepy ones. And the teacher's comfort may not be the most
important factor. People all have different comfort levels. One
child told a researcher, "A sweater is something my mother
makes me wear when she is cold."

Design of the room is another thing to observe. Some young
people are very comfortable in a formal setting. They like chairs
set up in rows. Others prefer to drape their bodies all over the
furniture. These seem to be biological needs that relate to kids'
physical well-being, and they *do* make a difference. Find out

158

what your child enjoys, and try to discover if some element in the room or missing from the room is causing problems.

Also find out how the class period is structured. Often in Sunday School most instruction takes place through lecture, yet only between two and four students out of a group of ten will learn best by just sitting and listening. Some learn through feeling and touching and body movement; others learn by a combination of senses. You need to find out what the teacher is doing and let the teacher know what kinds of things hold your child's interest.

Time of day also affects learning. People have varying energy levels during the day. Twenty-eight percent of elementary-age kids are early-morning persons, and they will usually get along just fine in Sunday School. But as people get older, the percentage of morning people drops. So if Sunday School is not exciting to your child because morning is not the best time of his day and he is still half asleep, you will have to lower your expectations. Because of his biological rhythms, he'd obviously rather be home in bed, or perhaps outside playing.

You can't expect the Sunday School to be eager to change all these factors to suit your child's needs, but you might be able to influence change in one or two areas. If you understand your child's particular needs, you will better understand why he relates to Sunday School as he does.

3. *Get acquainted with your child's Sunday School teacher.* Invite the teacher home for a personal evening with your family. During the Vietnam War, I was teaching Sunday School at an Air Force base in Japan. A lieutenant colonel's daughter who was in one of my classes invited me home to meet her parents. It was exciting to get to know her family in a natural setting. As the evening progressed, the girl went out to play with her friends, leaving me alone with her parents. It was an opportunity for them to hear about what our class was doing. At the end these non-churchgoers said, "Now we understand better why our daughter enjoys Sunday School so much." My evening with that family helped them know what was going on in their daughter's life, and it also helped me know how to relate to the girl better. Perhaps it also made them consider what church had to offer them.

I'm surprised that many parents don't take time to share vital information with the Sunday School teacher—not even as much as they would share with a babysitter or give to a day-school teacher. For example, a Sunday School teacher should be told if a student is in an accelerated class in school. Sunday School teachers want to offer more stimulation to such students. Tell the teacher what he or she needs to know, even if it is not all positive—"Billy bites when he's angry." In return, the teacher will feel more open to reciprocate with information about the student's performance and response—"Billy got mad at Jane today and didn't bite her. He said Jesus didn't want him to."

DON'T PANIC

Our children tend to pattern their lives after ours. Most often children accept the same church affiliation and political party as their parents. Rebellion is the exception rather than the rule, and it will seldom happen if the parents: (1) live consistent Christian lives, (2) attend church themselves and enter into church activities, (3) speak well of their pastor and the total church ministry, and (4) support the church with tithes and offerings.

Paul Kienel

---

4. *Reinforce Sunday School at home.* Most Sunday School curriculum is based on a thirteen-week quarter in which one theme is covered. This can be enhanced by home activities. For instance, if the children are studying Genesis one quarter, the family could visit a zoo to discover some of the strange and wonderful animals our Creator God has made. Or if they are studying about the Children of Israel in the wilderness wanderings, the family might make a model of the tabernacle to take to Sunday School class.

Life response is as important as Bible content. Parents can facilitate this by helping children learn to be less self-centered and to care about others, such as neighborhood shut-ins. Parents can help children prepare food baskets to give away at Thanksgiving; children can sing carols to the elderly at Christmas.

But what if your child's Sunday School really *is* boring? As much as we educators hate to admit it, this is sometimes really the case.

5. *Help the teacher improve her skills.* Can you invite the dull teacher along with you to visit an exciting classroom, perhaps at the school your child attends? Sometimes vibrancy and good ideas rub off. It is much easier to practice creative teaching methods when you have seen them in action. If you have observed a class doing mime or role play, it is much easier to adapt these activities to a Sunday School environment.

Pay a teacher's way to a local Sunday School convention, or offer to team teach with the teacher. Some teachers figure that if their only audience is a bunch of third-graders, they don't have to prepare or spend energy on too much organization. But if they know another adult is going to be there, they might get their act together.

It seems so simple, but we often forget to pray for our child's Sunday School teacher. Remember that teaching is a difficult job. She doesn't get paid, and she probably gets very few thank-yous for her work. Make the teacher a permanent name on your prayer list—and let her know of this prayer support.

Donate some good books on teaching to your church library. Or give the teacher one or two as a Christmas present—a subtle hint that learning goes on even for adults.

Sometimes you can encourage a teacher to individualize her teaching. Ask her to give your child personal assignments. These get the child involved in the topic that is being studied and in class interaction as he shares his findings. When a child brings something to class, he has an investment in making the class period succeed, even if the teacher is not highly successful.

These assignments work for adults as well as for children. It was easier for me to be involved in the worship service on Sundays when my husband and I had been part of a church planning group. I was more alert and involved when I had a chance to read the Scripture or a poem rather than just sitting down and waiting for the pastor to do the work.

6. *Consider changing churches.* Sometimes, even with hard work, the boredom won't go away. The teacher can't be changed, and the child's attitude toward God is being seriously

affected by the weekly boredom and apathy. When things get to this point, I honestly recommend that you change churches.

When I was a teenager, my parents chose their church on the basis of its fine Sunday School program for teenagers. They knew I needed it, and even though the church was not their personal preference, they attended it for me. They stayed with it until I went off to college, knowing I needed the support of a strong youth group during those important years. They did it for me, and that's exciting.

There is nothing more important than a Christian peer group for junior-high and high-school children. I have a friend whose father was pastor of three different churches while she was growing up. Because each was very small, she was without an ongoing Christian peer group. She was doing everything possible to become more like her secular friends. Fortunately, her father realized the problem. He quit pastoring for a few years and drove a meat truck in a small town instead. That way they could attend a church with lots of teens, and she could be part of a Christian youth group.

7. *Thank God for loving teachers.* Teachers who genuinely love and care about their children can make all the difference in the world in bringing these children to God. Such teachers reflect the love of Jesus Christ and serve as models even when their teaching is not polished or their grasp of methods flawless. This is the most important factor in preventing boredom and enhancing children's experience of God—teachers who love kids and who are open to growth themselves as they encourage their students to walk in the Lord.

Sunday Begins on Saturday Night
DAVID & KAREN MAINS

IN OUR FAMILY, WE HAVE TRIED TO CAPTURE THE MEANING behind our belief that Sunday morning at God's house is the high point of the week, the apex of our weekly experience. It is not a time to sit down and be as self-indulgent as possible, as many secular people seem to believe. Instead, it is a time to celebrate.

We have played games like the Sunday Search to make our

Sundays more meaningful. We have paid careful attention to church life. But we have found that Sunday, all by itself, is not enough.

After studying Scripture on this theme and observing Orthodox Jewish practices in Israel, we have concluded that we, like the Jews, really need to set aside two days instead of just one—a day to get ready and a day to celebrate.

From the time of the Exodus, the Jews named two special days of the week: the Sabbath (Saturday) and the Day of Preparation (Friday). But in Jewish thought, the idea of Sabbath is not limited to those two days. The Jewish week is set up so that there are three days of anticipation followed by the Sabbath, then three days to reflect on what happened on the Sabbath.

Before we began viewing Sunday in this new light, it had been a traumatic day with plenty of confusion and bustle. We had to start from scratch and go through a serious planning process in order to make the Lord's Day the focal point of our week.

In the Jewish week, the Sabbath begins at sundown the night before. We knew that, ideally, our preparation for Sunday morning church should begin Saturday night. But what usually happened? The kids had other plans. They were out late Saturday night on dates or at parties or being entertained. Of course, on Sunday morning they would wake up exhausted, unprepared to worship or make the most of the day. Even if they made it to services on time, they were tired and out of sorts.

So to make our Sunday mornings what they ought to be, we decided to change our Saturday nights. We now try to make Saturday evening the preparation time for Sunday worship. We encourage our children to use Fridays for socializing if possible. This is not a legalistic rule with us; if the kids can't avoid going out on Saturday night, we say, "Fine, but try to be home by 10 or so."

Then we single out a special Saturday evening every three weeks or so for a special Sabbath-like family celebration. We eat a meal together; we share what God has done in our lives; and David, the father, gives each child a blessing. This not only helps them get ready for Sunday; it also helps them realize our love for them through ritual and tradition, which is consistent with biblical practice.

One memorable celebration happened not long before Randy,

our oldest child, went to Mexico as a summer missionary. Everyone in the family got together one Saturday night. Each of us—grandparents and all—gave him a special blessing. One gave his blessing in the words of a song, which he read and then played while we sang. That was truly an electrifying moment, one Randy will not forget for the rest of his life.

We don't expect good results in our business activities or in our homemaking if we don't plan ahead. We carry datebooks and shopping lists; we prepare reports for tomorrow's important conferences; and we bake and freeze casseroles for dinners that won't happen until next week. Our day-to-day life is important to us, so we prepare for it.

But how much more important is our Christian life! We need to plan just as carefully for Sunday as we do for every other day. If we do, it can be the high point of the whole week.

CHAPTER
11

How Do I Help
My Child Stand Up for
His Convictions?

"Everyone's Doing It"
DAVID VEERMAN

"BUT EVERYBODY'S DOING IT!"

How often have parents heard this response by their teenagers answering or reacting to a restriction? Drinking, curfew, clothes, hairstyle, cheating, dating—all are fair game.

How should we as parents respond to this line of reasoning, considered almost "irrefutable"? First, it is important to ask *why* the argument is used—why it is so important to teens. One word helps our understanding—*security*. Adolescence is the age of identity, discovering "who I am and where I fit in." It is very threatening to be alone, to stand out from the crowd. The group and its morés mean everything.

Second, we must be honest about our own lifestyles. I'm afraid that adults are quite susceptible to group pressure. Tastes in clothes, cars, and even politics are fashioned by society. (Has anyone discovered a use for the necktie?) How often do *we* act on principles regardless of what people think? Confession is, "good for the soul" and also good for relationships. It will be helpful, therefore, to "fess up" to our tendencies.

Understanding the feelings behind the phrase and confessing our own failings, let us consider our possible answers.

It would be easy to counter with a quick retort or a dogmatic "No, because I said so!" But such a response is usually counterproductive. We may win the battle and lose the war. Instead, our answers should lead to deeper communication and teaching opportunities. In that light, then, here are some suggestions that are formed as questions to lead to further discussion:

- Is everyone *really* "doing it"? Who isn't? Why?
- When is "everyone" wrong? (Truth is often in the minority. Look at Christ.)
- What is more important: doing what is *right* or doing what everybody does?
- Are there groups of "everybodies" that you should avoid . . . or leave?
- Is "everybody" doing "it" because "everybody's doing it" or are there other reasons?
- Is it wrong to be different?
- How do *you* treat people who are different?
- Whose opinion is *most* important to you?
- Can *you* swim against the tide? Can you change what "everybody" is doing?

As we lead the discussion with gentleness and honesty, we help our young people develop their own values and the courage to do what is right regardless of what "everybody" is saying or doing.

Instilling Values That Will Last a Lifetime
JIM & SALLY CONWAY

DEVELOPING VALUE STANDARDS BEGINS BEFORE CHILDREN become teenagers. Beginning at birth, parents should use every situation that comes along to teach their children how to live life. You need to give them increasing amounts of responsibility and freedom to exercise choice.

Don't say to your child, "Do this because I say you should," or "I'm bigger than you," or "As long as you live in this house, you will do this." As soon as you use that method, you have a child who's functioning on the basis of parental values, not on the basis of his own values.

Children and teens need guidance and insight from their parents in order to form their values. Think about ways you can implement the following in your family:

1. From the beginning you need to talk about *why* you do things—why you keep your room clean, why you participate in family chores, why you don't lie, why you don't cheat. Simply saying, "Our family doesn't do that" is not good enough.

When the children become teenagers and go off to high school, their friends might say, "Let's go get drunk." At that point, saying "Our family doesn't do that" is not a good enough reason. A teen needs to be able to explain not only why his family doesn't drink, but also why he personally doesn't. An unprepared teen will be caught trying to stand up for family values that are not his own and will most likely end up giving in to peer pressure.

2. Before the teen years, help your children develop a reflective approach to life. They need to ask, "What is life about?" "Why am I doing this?" "Why don't I do this?" "Why do I think this way?" "What do I want to accomplish with my life?"

It helps to talk about an issue ahead of time. If you want them to think through whether or not they will ever drink, begin at an age when it isn't a problem. If the issue is whether or not they will have premarital sex, discuss it *before* they become emotionally involved with someone.

This kind of communication should take place during informal times. You don't have to have a special session to discuss the birds and the bees, especially when kids are exposed to so much so early on TV.

Perhaps an unmarried girl your children know has gotten pregnant. Parents can use that example, even with grade-school children, to teach why premarital sex is wrong. Do so in a way that does not condemn the person involved, yet lovingly explain why to avoid such a situation.

Most parents are so busy with daily survival that they forget the long-range goal of developing this individual to be a whole person as he steps into his teen years and adulthood.

3. Of course, as children grow and move along in school, aging helps to develop some degree of maturity. Life's experiences will automatically give them insight.

But along with life's experiences they need cognitive information. They need parents to provide some of that knowledge. In developing values, teens need a variety of ideas to work with. If they are working only with their own resources or those of their friends, they have very limited material.

Get them started reading early in life. *The Living Bible* and *Campus Life* magazine would be good resources for teens.

4. Parents can also provide *experiences* that will broaden their children's cognitive information. There's nothing quite like a week away at camp, where leaders will stimulate kids' minds to think through issues. They can wrestle with what to do about sex and how to relate to their parents.

Then, teens need opportunities to think and reflect by themselves. They need time to meditate, to sit out in the sun, under a tree, or in their rooms—just to think about life. It is important that teens are not always busy and "on the go" or wasting time watching TV. Parents can encourage teens to have reflection times.

When our family went camping, we would take a canoe into the middle of the lake at night so that everyone could quietly look at the stars. That is one way to encourage reflectiveness. Another way is to teach teens how to have a quiet time. As a family, read a section of Scripture and spend time reflecting on it, asking what it means for each person's life.

6. Teenagers also need a peer group for interaction. In a group they can throw ideas around, learning what others think. By sharing thoughts and getting feedback, they are forming values.

7. Stress often helps develop values. Parents often look at the teen years, which are high stress times, as bad times. But without stress there is little value development. Teens need to experience occasional pressures and difficulties. We're not doing our teens a favor by taking all the problems out of their lives. Remember, stress times are teachable times.

When life is coasting along, there is no pressure. There is little thinking either. Some parents try to shelter their children from ever having to face a decision or temptation. But a teen's values are strengthened through wrestling with issues and problems. The stresses of life provide opportunities for new learning and new development.

8. Parents should give their kids the freedom to fail. A teen can learn as much from failure as from success. Teens need to know that their parents are going to stand with them and not abandon them when they fail—not *if* they fail, but *when* they fail.

Of course, parents should not knowingly let their teens make mistakes that are going to alter their lives permanently. But a lot of Christian parents go overboard the other way, trying to protect their kids from ever making crucial decisions on their own.

Sometimes parents send their children to a Christian school,

"SHOW ME"

Teens fall into two categories. About 30 percent can be characterized as the proauthority group. They want approval and desire to please people in authority. Their needs for security, authority, and structure are naturally met by the promises of Christianity, and thus they are generally quite receptive to the Gospel.

Seventy percent of teenagers are antiauthority. They want to think for themselves, and seek to please themselves, not those in authority. They have a "show me" attitude. They are not receptive spiritually, and don't respond to pressure tactics. For these teens we need to be good examples. They are waiting to be shown the validity of our values. If they respect us and see our faith in action over a long period of time, they will gradually become receptive to Christianity.

Ross Campbell

---

thinking they are going to protect them from the world's problems. There are good reasons for sending your children to a

Christian school, but if your reason is to keep them away from the stresses of life, you are not helping them.

In fact, Christian schools should program stress and controversy so there is an opportunity for growth. Teens need to talk about issues and have their values deliberately questioned instead of just being told what to do.

9. Parents can help their teens recognize the difference between Christian standards and non-Christian standards. But you need to be realistic so your teens are not expecting to find evil behind every bush.

You also need to coach them that life is not all black and white. If teens are told that a movie is *totally* bad, they may see it and like parts of it. Then they begin to question their parents who told them it was awful. Parents need to show children that God has created people with a great deal of diversity. All things that are not Christian are not 100 percent evil.

10. Teach your teens to look at the world through Jesus' eyes, aware of the wrong but loving toward people. Virginia Satir, a noted family therapist, found that happy, secure, successful families have an open attitude to circles other than their own, and families in trouble tend to be suspicious and shut off from the world.

When our girls were in high school, they were friends with kids that we could never have had contact with because they weren't "our kind." Yet our daughters could be friendly with them and have an influence on them, even though they didn't participate in their drinking parties.

As a result, we have later met kids who made a decision for Christ based on the friendship they had with our daughters in high school. One boy told us he would drink at his locker during breaks between classes. Brenda's locker was near his. Her friendliness and accepting attitude of him as a person impressed him. When he got out of high school he accepted the Lord. He told us Brenda's life had greatly influenced that decision.

Parents need to realize that they won't always be around to help their teens stay straight. They can't ride in the backseat of the car while the teen is on a date. They can't be at parties, making all the decisions for the teen like they did when he was two years old.

11. The best thing you can do for your teens is to be a friend

and be available if they want another opinion or just want to talk. Say, "We know that you're going to be strongly influenced by your friends, but we'd like to give you another perspective from another generation if you would like to talk about it."

If you as parents haven't helped your teenagers to set values before adolescence, you need to admit that you have blown it. Explain, "We tried to *tell* you what to do instead of encouraging you to develop your own values." Then get started on helping them form values for themselves. It's late, but never too late. "One thing I do: Forgetting what is behind and straining toward what is ahead, I press on toward the goal to win the prize for which God has called me heavenward in Christ Jesus (Phil. 3:13-14, NIV).

Finding Stability in
a Changing World
LEIGHTON FORD

I WAS TALKING WITH A LOCAL YOUNG LIFE DIRECTOR A few years ago. He told me what frightened him most was that teens used to rebel over what they saw as their parents' hypocrisy. But now he just sees them weary and sad, as if they are saying, "Well, we didn't expect anything different." They are disillusioned with their parents and have given up expecting their parents to have strong values.

Young people today have more choices—more foods, more styles, more radio stations, more types of music, more kinds of movies—than ever before. These choices are available to parents too, but it is different for young people. They have grown up in a bewildering world where they not only have so many choices but must make them without the help of any absolute standard.

It's no wonder that a lot of teenagers today are so confused, with so many decisions to make and no guide by which to make them. Hans Selye, the famous Montreal doctor, who popularized the concept of stress, said that teenagers have always faced the stresses that we face today, with one exception: the stress of so many choices.

Years ago, a girl would do what her mother did; a son would do what his father did. But now we're faced with the smorgasbord effect. There are so many different options that commitment to one in particular becomes less and less important.

I walked through a shopping mall recently which featured every kind of shop imaginable. I walked through one store for thirty seconds, another one for two minutes, and I suddenly thought, "This is how many people treat life today. Two minutes for God, one minute for football, thirty seconds for morality."

I think if teens don't see a firm commitment on the part of parents, then they will look to other adult role models. They are desperate for guidance. They need to know that our values are based on something beyond what we were brought up to do, or just what we feel is right, or what society says.

One girl told me, "My father doesn't have sex with other women, but every ad he puts out has a sexy girl in it." Kids are very quick to pick up on that. If a parent comes home and has to have two or three martinis before dinner, and then talks about the dangers of marijuana or of the keg party, kids will see the discrepancy.

We have to reexamine our own standards as parents and ask if our lifestyles and values are founded simply on personal feelings and desires, handed down through social traditions, or squarely based on the standards of the God whose nature doesn't change.

The time we spend in the Bible is important. Do our teens see us reading it as well as obeying it? George Gallup says, "The fact is, despite the best efforts of our churches, our homes, and the religious media, we are producing today a nation of spiritually undernourished and religiously illiterate youth." One-fourth of all teens never read the Bible, fifteen percent can't name one of the Ten Commandments.

We have to have some rules. I remember asking our kids what would help them to develop their own character. Immediately our son, Kevin, replied, "Having some rules. I don't always like them, but I know I need them."

● *The anchor of God's Word.* Studying the Scriptures can help us discern the difference between what is cultural and what is from God. But it is even more helpful to study with a group of people because we tend to read our prejudices into the Bible. We also tend to want to change nothing or to go all the way and change everything. But we need a balance. Being part of a body of believers can help us look at ourselves honestly.

Learning to differentiate between our own prejudices and God's absolutes isn't always easy. God gave us His commandments, but we keep adding new ones. If we try to teach our own particular values, but can't give reasons for obeying them and can't ground them in the Word of God, then our teens aren't going to listen to us.

Someone once said, "You can't become a Christian without admitting you're wrong," but conversion is the last time a lot of Christians make such an admission. Being a Christian is to realize that we need constant repentance. God's Word is not wrong, but we may be wrong and may have to change.

Christ had all the answers and the Scriptures provided the authoritative guide, but we don't have all the answers just because we're Christians. That's humility. It is a willingness to be taught, to learn even from our kids. We need to be willing to look at new ideas, and not be afraid of changing the map of reality that we grew up with.

● *What kids want from their parents.* I was very impressed with something I read written by teens in a Canadian correctional institution. They advised parents: "Keep cool; don't lose your temper when things get rough. Kids need the reassurance that comes from controlled responses. Don't reach for the crutches of liquor and pills. We lose respect for parents who tell us to behave one way and then behave another. Be strict and consistent with discipline; keep the dignity of parenthood; we need someone to look up to. Finally, light a candle. Show us the way; tell us God is not dead or sleeping or on vacation. We need to believe in something bigger and stronger than ourselves."

Teaching Teens How to Make Right Decisions
JIM & SALLY CONWAY

TEENS NEED TO THINK THROUGH THE OUTCOMES OF THEIR decisions. By doing this, they become reflective people. It can begin with little things like choosing clothes or deciding whether or not to go to the football game. Then, when it comes to big decisions, they've had some practice using their judgment.

The kids we see who can't make good decisions by the time they reach their teenage years have been sheltered from thinking about every side of an issue. They've been told what their opinions should be. They have never thought through the consequences or been allowed to experience them.

One way to encourage children to make right decisions is to have them decorate their rooms. By this experience, they get practice in making decisions and learn how to live with the consequences. If they've painted their room purple with red stripes, they will have to live with it a while. They may change the colors eventually, but they've made the choice and have to put up with it.

If you have been building friendships with your children all along, you have a good foundation for sharing with each other when the time comes to make a major decision. There were times in each of our daughters' lives when it looked like they would become engaged to guys we weren't comfortable with.

Instead of saying, "You can't marry him," we had a good enough relationship that we could talk about our misgivings together. We'd discuss the fellow's good and bad points, and our daughters were free to say, "I really like him for this, but I have a problem with that."

One time, one of our daughters became rather defensive about a particular guy. She was really pushing us to accept him, and even though we didn't feel comfortable, we prayed that God would change us if this was the man for her. Then we began to accept him as much as we honestly could.

As soon as our daughter felt we were no longer resistant, she backed off and took a realistic look at him for herself. When she did, the relationship crumbled. If we had said at the beginning, "You have to quit seeing him; he isn't good for you," she would have worked all the harder to make him appear presentable.

There really are very few times when you have to step in and forbid something if you have a longstanding friendship and open communication with your teens. In a good relationship, you are sensitive to each other and are working together instead of taking sides.

It's time to shift roles from that of parent to that of friend when teens go off to college or begin to live outside the home. It becomes more complicated, however, if they are living at home while they work or go to school. Then you need to discuss the new relationship.

If your young adult children choose to stay at home for four or five years after high school, they may have to abide by some limits because they are using their parents' home. But parents also have the responsibility to realize that they have another adult in the house and should be careful not to interfere in their son's or daughter's decisions. Now is the time to enjoy each other as good friends.

When Can We Trust Our Teenagers?
JAY KESLER

YOUR TEENAGE DAUGHTER BREEZES INTO THE LIVING room and plants a loving kiss on your cheek. Casually she mentions that her room is spotless, homework done, the dishes have been cleaned up, and tomorrow there are no exams at school.

You glance quickly at your spouse, and without a word you ask each other, "What does she want?"

You don't have to wait long for an answer. "Mom and Dad, is it OK if Jim picks me up at 7:00? [It's 6:55.] A bunch of us are getting together tonight. I promise I'll be home by 10:00."

Staring at the bedroom ceiling, you lie awake waiting for your daughter's return. At 11:07, she tries to sneak through the back door, but of course you hear her. The worry is over, but with a sigh you wonder aloud, "When can we trust our kids?"

Do you know what trust involves? Do you know how to develop trust within yourself and within your children? These are difficult questions for all of us, and no one has all the answers. There are certain biblical guidelines, however, that relate to trust and that can help parents make good decisions.

1. *Get to know your children.* You do not trust someone you do not know. We must reach kids where they are, not where we wish they were. Earl Wilson, in his book, *You Try Being a Teenager,* explains it this way: "Without respect, there cannot be

175

love, and without love, there cannot be friendship (or trust). This friendship is much more than being chums with your son or daughter—it is in-depth knowing, caring, respecting. Be available to your kids. True friends play together, work, think and feel together, solve problems together, share dreams together, and interact with God together."

Some parents worry, "If we get too close to our kids, they'll walk right over us." In fact, the opposite is usually true. Parents maintain greater respect and authority in close, healthy relationships.

2. *Be an example.* Parents who are forced to say, "Don't do as I do; do as I say," lose the strong influence of a good example.

3. *Build their self-esteem.* It is a good idea to affirm in public and discipline in private. My collie will get up and walk the length of the yard for a pat on the head, and so will most of us. Kids are no exception. Be generous with your praise.

4. *Communicate with your kids.* Remember that communication is a two-way street. Teens won't share their inner feelings if they sense that their answers will be graded like an exam or ignored because the expected response wasn't given. By demonstrating a sincere interest in what your children say, you will begin to develop strong, lifelong relationships with them.

5. *Develop values in your children.* "Values and morals cannot be taught without consistent discipline," says Wilson. "By the time your children become teenagers you can no longer impose your values on them. The only alternative is to try to build a relationship with your teenagers in such a way that they see you as someone who is helpful to consult in developing values." Help your teens use their values when making decisions.

6. *Develop responsibility in your children.* Let your teenagers know that you want to give them more freedom and independence, but that in the process they must learn to take on more responsibility. For example, if your son has difficulty getting home on time, then he is not ready to take out someone else's daughter.

As your teenagers begin taking on more responsibility, make trust an automatic part of the process. Tell your teenagers that you trust them to take care of the car when they use it, or that you trust them to take care of the house when you are away for the weekend.

When teenagers leave home, the choices they make will be their own. Hopefully, your trust will have developed within them the character and independence they need in order to stand against things which don't agree with their values.

"WHY DON'T THE KIDS TRUST US?"

Trust is a valuable gift, and losing it is tragic. Unfortunately, however, the "trust-thread" is easily snapped. A broken confidence or a promise forgotten may destroy a friendship that took years to build.

Trust is a word often used in parent-teen relationships. The high schooler confronts with, "What's the matter; don't you trust me?" And Mom and Dad wonder why the kids don't confide in them like they did when they were younger.

This is a difficult area for parents to handle emotionally. They know the kids aren't taking their advice, and they feel threatened by their listening to and confiding in others.

This happens mainly because teenagers are trying to grow up and be "on their own," and this involves "apron-string-cutting." It may also be that they are afraid of disappointing or hurting Mom and Dad, so they don't tell them *everything.*

Often, however, parents exacerbate the problem through their actions. We may say one thing and then do another—inconsistency breeds mistrust. Or we overstate the case (e.g., an overprotective mom says, "If you kiss a boy, you'll get pregnant"). When the kids learn the facts, they also learn not to believe everything we say.

There are no easy answers to the trust question, but here are some suggestions:

1. We shouldn't confuse their desire for independence with a lack of trust in us.

2. We shouldn't try to be infallible. Instead, we can give our kids two *good* choices and let them choose.

3. We should be willing to tolerate conduct which differs from our own opinions (we expect *them* to do

this) and not hold it against them.

4. We should communicate honestly and on a *feeling* level (e.g., "You can do this, but I'm not for it"), again letting them know it won't be held against them.

5. We should hold confidences and *never* share their secrets with others.

YFC Editors

7. *Understand what it means to be a teenager.* Realize that to be young is to be different. To be young is to be in rebellion. To be young is to question and to test. It doesn't mean that your kids are hostile, or that they will leave the time-tested things permanently. It just means that they are trying to find their own set of values.

8. *Recognize the emotional turmoil caused by a changing body.* Complexion problems, small stature, protruding ears, dental flaws, and glasses are all factors that can affect young people. Most of us can look back at those struggles and laugh. But while we were going through them, there was no humor in the situation at all.

These tremendous physical changes put great emotional strain on your teens. They will be attracted to someone who is sympathetic. If you aren't, someone else will be.

9. *Understand and emphathize with your children's social lives.* The social area is the most threatening and fear-filled of all for many young people. Teenage society can be quite cruel. Often parents can't figure out why their kids are in one group when another looks so much more constructive. The truth may be that your children prefer the other group but have been rejected by it on an arbitrary basis such as looks.

10. *Discover your children's strong points.* Focus attention on those strengths. It is very difficult for trust to thrive in a negative atmosphere. This is not to say that we can never correct our kids. Pointing out failure is only effective, however, when kids are secure in our love and esteem.

These ten guidelines help us discover how to develop trust within a family atmosphere. If we put these guidelines to work, can trust become a regular part of our lives? Let's look at some specific examples.

Rather than dolling out money to kids, give them an allowance and trust them to have the ability to budget it according to their needs. It is important not to bail out your teens if they run short of cash. Let them go without until the following week when they again receive their allowance. Hopefully, they will learn how to do a better job of budgeting.

Help your teens to understand that they give account of their time as a matter of respect for others (so that no one will worry about them), rather than as a means for you to check up on them. Ask your teens, "How much time do you think you need after this school activity? What time do you think you should be in?" Demonstrate your faith in their ability to set some of their own time standards, but at the same time, make them stick to their commitments.

It is good for children to see the connection between responsible behavior and privilege. As they learn to be responsible in their actions, they should be given more privileges. This type of trust builds maturity.

Trust must be encouraged and reinforced, but keep in mind that your kids are not perfect. When kids fail, however, many parents make the mistake of removing all trust. They say, "We can't trust you again until you prove that you can be trusted." But if the children are not given trust, how can they prove that they are worthy of it? When parents say, "Earn my trust," they are actually demonstrating an attitude of distrust.

This attitude is unrealistic and unfair because your children may be very responsible in other areas of their lives. You may have to take away certain privileges for a time, but keep communication going. Tell your kids why these consequences are necessary. And as soon as possible, give them another opportunity to be responsible.

We must also be careful not to project our own bad performance onto our kids. For instance, fathers often feel that when their daughter goes on a date, they know just what the boy has on his mind. Now the truth is that they don't know at all what that boy has on his mind. All they know is what they had on their minds when they were seventeen. Many Christian kids wouldn't think of doing some of the things their parents did before they were saved. Everyone ought to get a chance to prove they are trustworthy.

Though we take the risk of being deceived, it is still more powerful to trust our children than to protect ourselves from being fooled. It is important for your children to know that your love for them is unconditional and unshakable even in the face of disappointment and fear.

Can you be certain everything will work out right? No, you can't. But remember that developing trust is like a baby learning how to walk. You must take the first difficult step toward a lasting relationship. There is risk of humiliation, failure, and rejection. As you demonstrate faith in your kids' abilities to act responsibly, as you step out to give them another chance, the effects of your trust begin to work. The results are slow and unsteady at first, but over time your family should reap the rewards.